Churchward Locomotives

Churchward Locomotives

A Pictorial History

Brian Haresnape
Alec Swain

LONDON
IAN ALLAN LTD

First published 1976

ISBN 0 7110 0697 0

© Brian Haresnape & Alec Swain 1976

Published by Ian Allan Ltd, Shepperton,
Surrey, and printed in the United Kingdom by
Ian Allan Printing Ltd.

Contents

Previous page: In early BR livery of lined black, with Gill Sans lettering on tank sides, No 4409 was photographed working a train from Craven Arms near Much Wenlock on September 10, 1949. This locomotive was withdrawn about 18 months later with the total mileage, since built, of 1,028,204 to its credit – the highest for the class. At this late date the engine still sported a tall safety valve bonnet; it never received outside steam pipes./*H. C. Casserley*

Left: Raking sunlight emphasises the rugged character of Star class 4-6-0 No 4049 *Princess Maud,* photographed at Shrewsbury, August 28, 1952, a year before withdrawal. In final form, with Castle type outside steampipes./*B. E. Morrison*

Foreword

I am old enough to remember the Great Western as it was between the years 1910 to 1920. I think the beautiful curves and double frames of the Dean engines appealed to me more than the angular lines of the Churchward engines, impressive as they were, and I recall as a child how very disappointed I was on changing into a Weymouth-Paddington train at Newbury, to find only a County tank at the head of it instead of a splendid Star as I had hoped, or a Dean Duke.

My old friend J. N. Maskelyne was a fanatical admirer of GWR practice. He regarded Churchward with veneration, and communicated this enthusiasm to me. Churchward was far less insular than his fellow engineers, and to bring over the wonderful De Glehn Atlantics was a stroke of great originality of thought, and to design the first English Pacific was another triumph, as she was a splendid engine in many ways. Of course Churchward had his blind spots, breaking up the old broad-gauge engine *North Star* and the only surviving true Sharp Single No 14 was certainly a tragedy.

I feel it a great honour to introduce this tribute to a great engineer, compiled by my two friends and fellow enthusiasts Brian Haresnape and Alec Swain. It is a fine tribute to a great and unique engineer.

J.E. Kite
Seaford, 1975

Introduction

The completion of a striking new 4-6-0 locomotive, No 100, at Swindon in February 1902 was to prove the keystone of the arch between Victorian and modern British steam design. Outwardly the locomotive was a dramatic departure from the stylistic 'signature' of William Dean, although that much revered gentleman still held office as Locomotive, Carriage and Wagon Superintendent of the Great Western Railway. Indeed, the severe lines and unquestionably American features of No 100, shocked the enthusiasts of the day, because they represented such a dramatic change from the established conventions. This locomotive heralded the dawn of the most exciting phase of locomotive development on the GWR and gave a positive indication of the manner in which Dean's chosen successor, George Jackson Churchward, intended to apply himself to the task of modernising Swindon locomotive practice.

Locomotive No 100 marked the commencement of ten years' steady development by Churchward, which was to result in a fleet of standardised modern steam locomotives without parallel in Britain at the time, and in the establishment of sound practices which were to influence later designs by other engineers. Since 1896, when Churchward had taken over as Works Manager at Swindon, a succession of experimental engines had appeared which were, in the main, concerned with improvement to the design of the boiler and smokebox. Some extraordinary looking engines were produced, which retained the massive outside frames that had characterised the products of Dean at Swindon for many years. Although Dean was still in the chair, his health was failing, and Churchward was called upon to take increasing responsibility for the jobs in hand. In 1898 he had been appointed chief assistant to Dean and this was taken as a fair indication that in due course he would be his successor. This event took place on June 1, 1902 – four months after the emergence of No 100 – when Churchward was 45 years old. A thoughtful gesture by Churchward was to name No 100 *Dean*, later *William Dean*, soon after the retirement of his old chief.

With inside frames and outside cylinders, a domeless parallel Belpaire boiler and high side platforms with the cab perched on the end in American style, No 100 could fairly be described as an Anglicised version of a contemporary American 'ten-wheeler'. Churchward's obvious awareness of trans-Atlantic trends might have been due in part to his friendship with A. W. Gibbs of the Pennsylvania Railroad, but was also fostered by the close study made at Swindon of the technical descriptions which apppeared in the journals of the day. Despite this early influence, Churchward also made a close study of Continental practices, for he was above all a broad-minded man, able to accept that other people's ideas might well be superior to those established at Swindon over the years. His principal aim was to produce locomotives very much superior to those running at the time, in order to meet the foreseeable demands of the Operating Department and customers. To achieve this he visualised the use of a range of standardised components, usuable in a range of standard locomotive types. So well did he succeed in this that not only were his engines able to meet all requirements during his 20 years in office, but also, in broad concept, they sufficed until the demise of steam on the GW lines.

In 1901, before taking full control, he produced an outline plan for six projected standard locomotive types (See Table 1) of which No 100 was the prototype. Because a period of development and proving in service was necessary at the outset of such an ambitious plan, Churchward also continued the construction of the Dean 4-4-0s for use on the accelerated express services, at the same time introducing progressive improvement to their boiler design and other details.

For his new standard range he produced a limited number of entirely new designs of boiler, cylinders, valves, valve gear and motion which could be utilised for a variety of new types in which the main variant would be the size and number of coupled driving wheels, pony trucks or bogie. Churchward's policy was to construct a prototype for each of the new types and thoroughly to prove it in service before embarking upon quantity manufacture. In this way, by 1905, he had amassed enough experience to proceed with confidence. It could be argued that if he had waited a little longer it is possible he would have used superheating from the outset, and possibly outside Walschaerts valve gear as by the end of the decade both features were proved in service on other railways.

One American feature that Churchward did not apply to No 100 was the use of bar frames, which would have added too much weight to the engine, but he compromised by using an American-style front end, with outside cylinders, an integral cast saddle and forged steel extension frames, bolted to the main plate frames. Great attention was paid to the design of the steam passages and cylinders, and a characteristic of Churchward practice emerged with the proportioning of the cylinder dimensions, in which a small diameter was adopted and the stroke of the pistons

Table 1
Churchward's 1901 outline scheme for six standard locomotive classes.

Type	2-8-0	4-6-0	4-6-0	2-6-2T	4-4-2T	4-4-0
Engine	97	—	100	99	2221	3473
Date of first engine,	June 1903	—	Feb 1902	Sept 1903	Dec 1905	May 1904
BOILERS:						
Length of barrel	15ft 0in	15ft 0in	15ft 0in	11ft 2in	11ft 2in	11ft 2in
Diameter of barrel	5ft 0in	5ft 0in	5ft 0in	5ft 0in	5ft 0in	5ft 0in
Length of firebox,	9ft 0in	9ft 0in	9ft 0in	8ft 0in	8ft 0in	8ft 0in
Length of connecting rods,	10ft 8½in	10ft 8½in	10ft 8½in	6ft 10½in	6ft 10½in	6ft 10½in
Wheels, diameter,						
Pony or bogie,	3ft 3in	3ft 3in	3ft 3in	3ft 3in	3ft 3in	3ft 3in
Coupled,	4ft 7½in	5ft 8in	6ft 8½in	5ft 8in	6ft 8½in	6ft 8½in
Radial	—	—	—	3ft 3in	3ft 3in	—
Cylinders	One pattern for all types, 18in diameter X 30in stroke with 8½in diameter piston valves.					

lengthened accordingly. The boiler design was an enlarged version of the domeless Belpaire type he had developed on the Dean 4-4-0s and 2-6-0s, and an important feature was the use of Stephenson's valve gear for the 6ft $8\frac{1}{2}$in driving wheels.

The stage was thus set. The action was to be both impressive and unhurried. In 1903 two further prototype 4-6-0s appeared, Nos 98 and 171, and some significant improvements were incorporated in them — in particular, in the design of the boiler and cylinders. The boiler, although somewhat similar to that designed for No 100, had a tapered section at the rear, uniting the barrel and the raised Belpaire firebox, with the aim of getting free water circulation at the hottest part of the firebox. Churchward saw the need for very free exhaust of steam, and the cylinders were improved with enlarged steam ports and piston valves of $10\frac{1}{2}$in diameter and long travel.

For express passenger duties there was some debate as to the preference for 4-4-2 or 4-6-0 wheel arrangement, and it is entirely characteristic of Churchward's open-minded attitude that he produced basically identical engines of both wheel arrangements, in order to make proper comparisons in service. Further questions arose regarding the validity

of compounding, which had produced excellent results on the Continent and had also been tried on American railroads. To settle the debate he obtained authority to purchase three De Glehn-Du Bousquet four-cylinder compound 4-4-2s from France, modified only in minor detail to suit the GWR loading gauge and so on. The first of them, No 102 *La France*, was tried against his own two-cylinder simple 4-6-0 design, and he modified No 171 *Albion* as a 4-4-2 in order to be more closely comparable. The question of four cylinders or two remained, however, and therefore he went a stage further and produced No 40 *North Star* as a four-cylinder simple 4-4-2, which was tried against the two later, and larger, French

Table 2
Churchward's Standard Scheme (as developed and including projected designs.)

Standard cylinders with 30in stroke and 10in valves.

Type	Coupled Wheel Dia	Std Boiler No	Class	Notes
4-4-0	6ft 8½in	4	3800	
4-4-0	6ft 8½in	2	(3805)	No 3805 ran thus from 1907-9
2-6-0	5ft 8in	4	4300	
2-6-0	5ft 8in	2		Not considered after the introduction of 4300.
4-4-2	6ft 8½in	1	2900	Altered to 4-6-0
4-6-0	6ft 8½in	1	2900	
4-6-0	6ft 8½in	7		Projected 1919
4-6-0	5ft 8in	1	(6800)	Projected 1901. Not built until 1936*
2-8-0	5ft 8in	1	(4700)	4700 as built; altered to No 7 boiler.
2-8-0	5ft 8in	7	4700	
2-8-0	4ft 7½in	1	2800	
2-8-0	4ft 7½in	7		Projected 1919.
4-4-2T	6ft 8½in	2	2221	

* Collett Grange class 4-6-0

Type	Coupled Wheel Dia	Std Boiler No	Class	Notes
4-4-2T	6ft 8½in	4	(2230)	2230 as built; too heavy, unless 4-4-4T adopted. Projected about 1905.
4-4-4T	6ft 8½in	4		
2-6-2T	5ft 8in	2	3111	
2-6-2T	5ft 8in	4	3150	
2-8-0T	4ft 7½in	4	4200	
2-8-0T	4ft 7½in	5		Projected during 1905-10 period.
2-8-2T	4ft 7½in	1		Projected 1905 but 2-8-0T adopted instead.
2-8-2T	4ft 7½in	4	7200	

4 cylinders with 26in stroke and 8in valves.

Type	Coupled Wheel Dia	Std Boiler No	Class	Notes
4-4-2	6ft 8½in	1	(40)	40 as built; altered to 4-6-0.
4-6-0	6ft 8½in	1	4000	
4-6-0	6ft 8½in	7		Projected 1919; too heavy until 1927.

Standard cylinders with 24in stroke and 8in valves

Type	Coupled Wheel Dia	Std Boiler No	Class	Notes
4-4-2T	5ft 8in	5	4600	
2-6-2T	4ft 7½in	5	4500	
2-6-2T	4ft 1½in	5	4400	
0-8-0T	4ft 1½in	5		Projected about 1905.

engines Nos 103 and 104. Once the debates were finally settled in favour of the 4-6-0 arrangement, and against compounding, for British conditions, the famous Star class four-cylinder simple 4-6-0 express passenger engines were produced.

The standard range of engines could therefore be finalised, as seen in Table 2. To this list may be added two solitary locomotives which were probably envisaged as part of the standard range, but which were not subsequently increased in number, or developed. The first was the magnificent Pacific No 111 *The Great Bear* of 1908, mainly built for prestige purposes, which was far ahead of its time and was severely limited by route availability problems. The second was the most attractive little light suburban tank engine, 4-4-2T No 4600, of 1913, which quite simply did not demonstrate any tangible advantages over his own excellent 4500 2-6-2Ts. Two projected designs which might have been envisaged as extensions to the standard range, but which did not materialise, were the outside-cylinder 0-8-0T pannier tank for shunting, with boiler, cylinders and wheels of the 4400 class; and the modified County Tank proposal which envisaged a 4-4-4T arrangement in order to carry the larger standard No 4 boiler. Several other suggestions, including one for a light 2-8-0T, were dropped when it became obvious that the existing new standard designs were sufficiently versatile.

In common with many great men in all

walks of life, Churchward was not immediately recognised by his contemporaries, and the full nature of his work on the steam locomotive went unheeded for some time. His development of the taper boiler, and cylinders, was advanced for the period, and he was criticised on the grounds of cost. His reputation was considerably enhanced by the results of the exchange trials of 1910, when his Star class 4-6-0 No 4005 *Polar Star* ran from Euston to Crewe competing against LNWR Experiment class No 1455 *Herefordshire*, while No 4003 *Lode Star* competed with No 1471 *Worcestershire* on GW metals. The Star design demonstrated masterly superiority over the LNWR engines, but the full reasons were not comprehended at Crewe. It was to be many years before the lessons of Churchward were brought to Euston by William Stanier, when he embarked upon the mighty restocking of the LMSR with a new range of standard designs in the Churchward tradition.

The Edwardians were proud of their steam locomotives and a great deal of thought went into their design, liveries and cleanliness. As already mentioned, Churchward came in for some severe criticism over the stark appearance of his prototypes, which was in no small degree due to their American influence. Although he remained very firm in his conviction that appearance considerations could not be allowed to hinder mechanical development, he did relent to the degree of instructing one of his draughtsmen, H. Holcroft, to improve the lines of his later engines and thereby produced – in the first series of Star class 4-6-0s – some of the cleanest and best proportioned large steam locomotives ever to run. It seems that the traditional GWR brass embellishments did not greatly appeal to him, and he made an attempt to do away with the copper chimney cap; but his attitude must have softened as time went by because all those features returned, although the austerity measures necessitated by World War 1 enforced a reversion to a plainer appearance for a while.

By 1916, when Churchward's title was altered to Chief Mechanical Engineer, his allotted task was almost complete. He had established a fleet of new locomotives which was to number no fewer than 888 by the time he retired at the end of 1921. The taper boiler had been steadily improved, with top feed and superheating, and he was still making headway in this field. In retrospect he is sometimes criticised for retaining low-degree superheat, but it should be remembered that he was responsible for a big advance in boiler pressure from the conventional 160-180lb psi to 225lb psi, besides introducing the modern superheated engine to this country. It was left to later engineers to build upon his solid foundations.

The final design to appear during the Churchward régime was of additional interest in that the boiler produced for it (after the prototype No 4700 had run for some time with a standard No 1 boiler) was a new standard No 7. The wheel arrangement was 2-8-0, with 5ft 8in coupled wheels, and the design was intended for fast running with vacuum-braked freights. The idea was prompted, in part at least, by the success of *The Great Bear* when employed on the 'Cocoa Train' between Bristol and London (so named because it conveyed the products of the Fry's chocolate factory) which prompted the traffic department to develop the concept of one-day transits between important towns. The 4700s were fine engines, and the big boiler was an excellent addition to the standard range. Churchward envisaged extending the use of the big boiler for an enlarged version of the Star class, an enlarged Saint and an enlarged 2800 heavy freight locomotive, all to cope with the probability of future requirements for larger and more powerful engines. His scheme was thwarted by existing civil engineering limitations which did not permit the maximum axle load of $20\frac{1}{2}$ tons that the two 4-6-0 designs would have had, and the schemes were not pursued beyond the outline diagram stage.

Churchward dealt mainly with the larger locomotive requirements, for all categories from express passenger to heavy mineral traffic, with the excellent 4300 class Moguls for mixed-traffic duties. He did not make a significant contribution to what was, by far the most numerous category of GWR locomotive, namely, the 0-6-0T, and although he was responsible for the change from saddle tank to pannier very few were actually fitted in his time. His successors, C. B. Collett and F. W. Hawksworth produced between them a further 1250 locomotives of Churchward standard design, modified only in minor details.

The undoubted excellence in service of the standard classes fully justified the pride which developed at Swindon and which survives today in the work of various active preser-

vation groups. It is not the aim of this book to present detailed analyses of locomotive performances, which have in any case been ably chronicled over the years. Nor are such subjects as accidents or mishaps dwelt upon. The object of this present work — the third in a series of pictorial histories of the locomotives of 20th century British engineers — is to present, in pictorial format, the general story of the Churchward engines. In addition to reviving many fond memories, I hope the illustrations will offer a clearer picture of the developments that took place. Fortunately the entire locomotive history of the Great Western Railway has been magnificently chronicled in 12 parts, by the Railway Correspondence and Travel Society (See Bibliography, page 112) and the reader desiring deeper technical knowledge is referred to this source. Quite recently a splendid *Locomotive Biography* featuring G. J. Churchward has appeared, written by Col H. C. B. Rogers, which gives a great deal of background information. I have therefore attempted to avoid unnecessary duplication of biographical detail.

Not everyone at Swindon it seems was convinced that Churchward's views on locomotive design represented progress. It speaks much for his confidence and broad-minded outlook that he allowed the rebuilding of Badminton 4-4-0 No 3297 *Earl Cawdor* in 1903 in a form which incorporated a number of ideas that were almost the antithesis of his own practice. A large round-top boiler, smokebox and small chimney of faintly Great Eastern aspect and a commodious cab of North Eastern style with double side windows, certainly altered the engine's appearance. In service it did not demonstrate any superiority, and before losing the large boiler, in 1906, the cab was altered to Churchward pattern./*Ian Allan Library*

No greater tribute can be paid to Churchward than to observe that his designs lasted until the final days of steam on the Western Region of British Railways, and in addition, that the range of standard locomotive types produced by BR owed a great deal to Churchward practice, as developed by Stanier, Ivatt, and Riddles. On the Southern Railway, Maunsell took note of Swindon developments and on the LNER Gresley benefitted from the adoption of long-travel valves. Perhaps the nicest touch of all was the bestowal of the name *Evening Star* [which had been carried by a GWR broad-gauge locomotive, then Churchward's Star class 4-6-0 No 4002] upon BR 9F 2-10-0 No 92220 – the last steam locomotive constructed at Swindon and the last new steam locomotive built for British Railways.

So far I have made no mention of Churchward's personal life. As already mentioned, an excellent biography has recently been published, but I would like to include the following extract from *Great Western Railway Magazine*, January 1934.

Death of Mr G. J. Churchward

It is with the deepest regret that we have to record the death of Mr George Jackson Churchward, CBE, MInstCE, MIMechE, who was from 1902 to 1921 Chief Mechanical Engineer of the Great Western Railway.

By the irony of fate it was the railway which claimed him in death, as it had in life, for he was struck and instantly killed just outside the grounds of his house, at Swindon, by the engine of the down Fishguard express, on Tuesday, December 19, about 10.20am. Exactly how the accident occurred will never be known, but Mr Churchward had left his house for his morning walk alongside his garden fence, which is only a few feet from the

Two projected Churchward designs which did not materialise. The outside-cylinder 0-8-0T pannier tank of 1905, and the 4-4-4T version of the County Tank with large boiler.

railway. No one appears to have witnessed the tragedy, but his badly mutilated body was found by the chargeman of a platelaying gang soon after the express had passed.

Mr Churchward was well known in engineering circles all over the country, and in his time was also looked upon, not only in this country but abroad as one of the leading authorities on locomotive practice. In addition, he occupied a unique position in Swindon by reason of his municipal activities.

An articled engineering pupil with the South Devon Railway, Mr Churchward was transferred to Swindon upon the amalgamation of that railway with the Great Western, in 1876, and passed through the drawing office before being appointed assistant manager in the carriage works in 1882. He subsequently became, in turn, assistant and manager of the locomotive works until, in June 1902, he was appointed Chief Mechanical Engineer. This post he held until his retirement in December 1921.

During his term of office, in addition to paying great attention to the standardisation of boilers and interchangeability of parts, his design of 4-cylinder 6-coupled express passenger engines placed the Great Western Railway in the forefront of locomotive practice in Great Britain.

In his capacity as a townsman, Mr Churchward was equally enthusiastic, and upon the establishment of the New Swindon

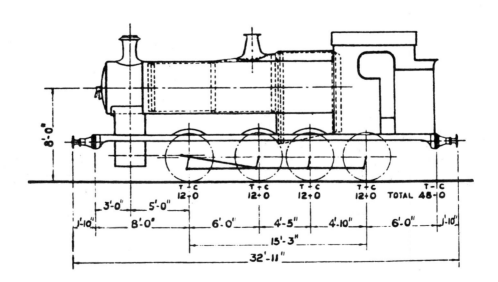

Urban District Council in 1894, he was elected a member of the Board, becoming Chairman in 1897. He was also a member of the Water Board from its commencement, and was the first Chairman of the Technical Education Committee, which was set up in 1898. When the Borough was incorporated, Mr Churchward became the first Mayor of the Borough of Swindon in 1900; and for his valuable services to the town as the first Mayor of the Borough and in other public offices; the distinguished position which he holds in the engineering profession, and the long and eminent services which he has rendered as head of the Great Western Railway works, Swindon, having attained success in all these spheres by the conspicuous ability and diligence at all times displayed by him' he was created the first Honorary Freeman of the Borough of Swindon in October, 1920.

There was, perhaps, no service Mr Churchward rendered more useful than his activities in the interest of higher education in Swindon, and the young men, in particular, owe a great deal to his zeal and foresight on their behalf. Upon his retirement from the railway service, his last act in this direction was to request that the bulk of the testimonial fund should be handed over in trust for the provision of annual grants to apprentices and junior clerks who distinguished themselves in their studies.

Mr Churchward was a great fisherman, and greatly prized a rod and outfit which were presented to him upon his retirement. He also regarded the gun with great affection and, although he was naturally proud of his county, Devon, and his birthplace, Stoke Gabriel, he loved the open rolling downs of Wiltshire. It was his wish that he should be buried in the churchyard of the Parish Church at Swindon.'

Throughout the preparation of this work I have had the constant assistance and advice of my co-author, Alec Swain, who is himself a Western Region motive power man besides being an ardent enthusiast. Together we have sorted hundreds of photographs, many taken by now unknown photographers (if only they had bothered to write the details and their names on the back!) and many taken by well-known camera artists. The final selection has been influenced mainly by the need to illustrate specific details. For assistance with illustrations we would like to thank the following: A.B. MacLeod; H.C. Casserley; J.E. Kite; Lens of Sutton; and J. Davenport. The line drawings are reproduced by courtesy of the *Railway Gazette* and Ian Allan Ltd, and the valuable services of the Ian Allan Library are gratefully acknowledged.

Brian Haresnape FRSA NDD
Box Hill, Surrey
June 1975

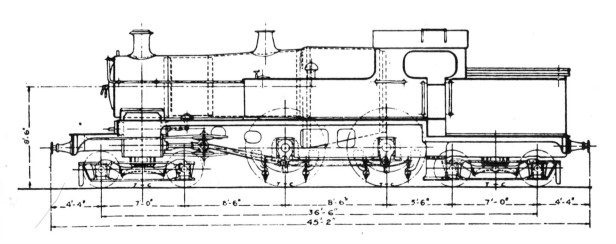

The Dean/Churchward Transition

A pictorial summary of the influence gradually brought to bear upon Swindon locomotive design by Churchward, during the period from his appointment as Chief Assistant to William Dean in September 1897, to his succession to the post of Locomotive, Carriage & Wagon Superintendent, upon Dean's retirement in May 1902, and his first years in that office.

This period witnessed a painstakingly thorough modernisation of boiler design, applied to what were basically still Dean locomotives, of late Victorian robust concept. Stage by stage Churchward initiated improvement, frequently by rebuilding, culminating in the highly successful large 4-4-0s which provided the mainstay of GWR express passenger power while his own new range of standard classes was under development, trial and quantity construction.

Right: Perhaps the earliest tangible example of Churchward's influence upon design was seen in the last-minute decision to incorporate Belpaire fireboxes, in place of the intended raised round-top type in the Badminton class of 1897. The first 18 of the class built, Nos 3292-3309, had domed boilers, but No 3310 *Waterford* emerged with his second domeless prototype Standard No 2 boiler, as illustrated. It had a steel firebox and Ramsbottom safety valves surmounted by a lever. The cab roof extended backward flush with the cab sides and was linked by pillars. The large combined name and numberplates on the cab sides also incorporated the builder's plates./*Ian Allan Library*

Below right: No 3352 *Camel* of the 3300, or Bulldog class, was the first locomotive to appear with a domeless prototype standard No 2 boiler with Belpaire firebox. Previously Duke class 4-4-0, No 3312 *Bulldog* had been constructed with the first prototype standard No 2 boiler, which, however, carried a dome. *Camel* was built in 1899 and shows the beginnings of Churchward influence upon Dean's designs. Other features of interest are the experimental numberplates on the smokebox sides (with number duplicated on the oval cabside plates) and special chimney with slight increase of diameter at band level. A smokebox ash chute is visible below the smokebox door. For some years these engines were referred to as the Camel class./*Ian Allan Library*

Above: One of Dean's final essays in steam locomotive design was this inside-cylinder 4-6-0, No 36, constructed at Swindon in August 1896. The first example of its wheel arrangement to appear on the GWR (indeed, one of the earliest to appear in Britain) it was a far cry from the 4-6-0s produced by Churchward in the ensuing decade. No 36 only lasted until the end of 1905 and seldom strayed far from Swindon during its brief career, which was mainly spent working trains on the Severn Tunnel line. Essentially a freight locomotive, No 36 (nicknamed the Crocodile) had 4ft 6in coupled wheels; double frames with inner members which terminated at the front of the firebox (which was unusually wide for a design of the period); and a bogie of Dean type with inside frames and inside swing links, which had wheels with Mansell wood centres – the Victorian double frame concept stretched to its limits./*Ian Allan Library*

Above: The Atbara class was built with parallel standard No 2 boilers and straight frames and was basically similar to the Bulldogs except for a coupled wheel diameter of 6ft 8½in compared to the 5ft 8in of the latter. The straight frames and cast-iron chimney certainly emphasised the Churchward angularity in design when compared to the flowing curves of the Dean era. Construction of this type, with progressive improvement in boiler design, proceeded steadily, while Churchward was hard at work on the design of his new-generation motive power. The Flower class of 1908 was similar to the Atbaras (which by then carried coned boilers) but had deepened stronger frames. Atbara No 3387 *Roberts* is seen, adorned for a special train conveying the City Imperial Volunteers. The size of the lumps of coal in the tender is quite remarkable./*Ian Allan Library*

Top right: A monstrous essay in locomotive appearance! The ugly Kruger, as it was nicknamed, appeared from Swindon in 1899. No 2601 was intended for the South Wales coal traffic and had 4ft 7½in coupled wheels, double frames above which

were mounted coil and volute springs, and a leading bogie with outside swing links. The forward part of the Belpaire firebox was a combustion chamber, while a single huge sandbox was saddled across the leading end of the domeless boiler. This engine was a development of Dean's 4-6-0 No 36 but it differed widely in many respects and showed that Churchward's preoccupation with boiler design was still in a very experimental phase./*Ian Allan Library*

Right: The prototype Aberdare appeared in August 1900 and was a much neater engine than the Kruger, as this splendid works photograph shows. This was a compact design compared to the Dean 4-6-0 and the Kruger, and was lighter. The design was based upon the Atbara and Camel 4-4-0s, with straight-top double frames. The boiler and smokebox, cylinders, motion and axles were all in common with those of the 4-4-0s. No 33 proved very successful in service, which was perhaps to be expected, as the parts had already been well tried on the passenger engines./*British Rail*

Left: The year 1900 also saw the introduction of No 11, a prototype 2-4-2T, or double-ender, for branch and local passenger working. No 11 had Webb radial axleboxes at the outer ends and with its single inside frames and fully enclosed cab it was an advance in GWR tank engine practice. Two-way steam-operated water pick-up apparatus was fitted, but this soon gave trouble because inadequate air vents caused the tanks to split open when water was picked up at too high a speed. The vents were consequently increased in size, as seen in the illustration of No 3611. The prototype and Nos 3601-20, which followed, had piston valves like those of the Krugers when new; later these were replaced by slide valves. The boiler was Churchward's domeless Belpaire, a shortened version of the No 2, which was designated standard No 3. The 2-4-2Ts were the only class to be built with these new boilers; the boilers were later passed on to 3521 class 4-4-0 rebuilds./*Ian Allan Library*

Centre left: The second Kruger locomotive emerged as a 2-6-0, with a pony truck unaesthetically placed well forward of the coupled wheels. The leading drivers had laminated springs in place of coil, but the volutes were retained for the other coupled wheels. A further eight locomotives were built in 1903 and the change to steam sanding, with boxes below the footplate, certainly cleaned up their appearance a little. Nos 2601/2 had this form of sanding fitted at about the same time. The final locomotive, No 2610, is seen here, photographed from an angle which emphasises the unhappy marriage of Churchward engine and tender of Dean origin. Compared to the Aberdare design these engines were not satisfactory in everyday service and had an extremely brief life, being replaced by an equal number of new Aberdares./*Ian Allan Library*

Bottom left: Although Dean was still in office when No 100 was introduced in February 1902, there can be no doubt, in retrospect, that this engine was Churchward inspired. The outside two-cylinder layout and Belpaire firebox with domeless boiler foreshadowed the trends to be followed in the ensuing 20 or so years. This immaculate official photograph was taken when the locomotive was just out of works, prior to receiving the name *Dean* – a thoughtful gesture by the GWR – which later, in 1902, was altered to *William Dean*. The original boiler was parallel and was replaced by a short-cone standard No 1 in June 1903. As built, No 100 had two cylinders of 18in diameter by 30in stroke and double-ported piston valves of $6\frac{1}{2}$in diameter. The valves were later enlarged to 7in and finally $7\frac{1}{2}$in. The total heating surface was 2410.31sq ft, which consisted of a tube heating surface of 2252.37sq ft and a firebox heating surface of 157.94 sq ft. The grate area was 27.62sq ft and boiler pressure was 200lb psi. The coupled wheel diameter was 6ft $8\frac{1}{2}$in and the bogie wheels were 3ft 2in. The engine weighed 67 tons 16cwt and the tender (which was of Dean pattern, with coal rails) weighed 43tons 3cwt, giving a total weight in working order of 110tons 9cwt./*British Rail*

Below: Further locomotives of the Aberdare type followed in 1901, and construction proceeded steadily until 1907, by which time 81 examples were in service. In September 1902 No 2661 emerged new, fitted with a parallel standard No 4 boiler. It was followed by Nos 2662-80 with coned No 4 boilers. Nos 2601-20 were also built new with the larger boiler, which gradually replaced the No 2 boilers on the earlier engines. As with all Churchward's boilers, steady improvement and development took place over the years, with the addition of superheating and top feed. No 2626 is seen in the original condition of 1901, with parallel No 2 boiler, cast-iron chimney and tall safety valve bonnet./*Ian Allan Library*

Top: Atbara class 4-4-0 *Mauritius* was rebuilt with a larger standard No 4 boiler in September 1902 and thus became the first of the famous City class. Ten new locomotives were delivered in 1903 and a further nine Atbaras were rebuilt in 1907-9. The City engines represented the peak of Churchward's development of the Dean inside-cylinder double-frame 4-4-0, but they were soon to be displaced from the principal express trains, which they worked so well, by the new generation of Churchward outside-cylinder designs. No 3435 (later 3712) *City of Bristol* is illustrated in original condition with slender cast-iron chimney, tall safety valve bonnet, and tender of improved design, with a fender in place of the coal rails. No 3717 *City of Truro* created a stir in the railway world of 1904 with a claimed top speed of 102.3mph descending Whiteball, an unparalelled performance for years to follow. Happily the locomotive was subsequently preserved (in later superheated form) by the company. It is now in Swindon Museum./*Ian Allan Library*

Above: A good example of the fertile and progressive work undertaken by Churchward in the quest to improve boiler design is this later picture of No 3310 *Waterford* after the locomotive had been rebuilt with a standard No 4 boiler in 1903. This led to all but three of the Badmintons being similarly rebuilt. Standard name and numberplates were used in the rebuild of No 3310, but the engine retained its unusual pillared cab. Some alteration was made to frames to strengthen them to carry the heavier boiler. In fact, considerable design effort was put into improving the frames of the Dean-inspired 4-4-0s, and the early curved variety, as seen here, were superseded by straight frames, which in turn were deepened and strengthened by Churchward. In this reboilered form the Badmintons were the equal of the Cities./*Ian Allan Library*

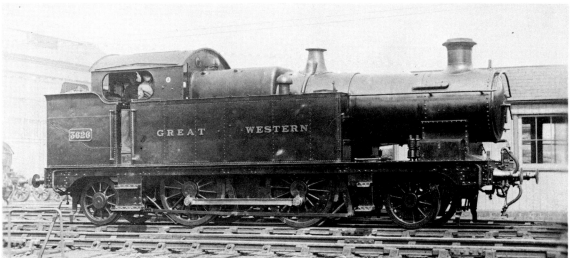

Top: Another interesting example of the latter-day appearance of one of the Dean/Churchward engines. No 3357 *Trelawny*, still carrying the oval cabside combined name and numberplates; photographed at Torquay. Originally No 3369 of the 3300, or Bulldog class, No 3357 is seen carrying a superheated No 2 boiler with top feed, and a tapered cast-iron 1920 pattern chimney on the extended smokebox. *Trelawny* was withdrawn from service in 1934, but two examples of the class, *Seagull* and *Skylark*, survived until November 1951./*C. C. B. Herbert*

Above: No 3626, a double-ender tank in latter-day condition, with the standard No 3 boiler fitted with superheater and top feed, and with extended smokebox. These 2-4-2Ts were superseded by the Churchward outside-cylinder 2-6-2Ts. The No 3 boilers were transferred to 3521 class 4-4-0s as they were 9in shorter in the barrel than the standard No 2 boilers. The remaining surplus was used on Bulldog 4-4-0s from 1933 onwards, and the 14 engines fitted had a backward extension of the smokebox to accommodate the shorter barrel./*Ian Allan Library*

The French Locomotives

Churchward was extremely alive to developments in locomotive design both on the Continent and in America. His own two-cylinder 4-6-0 prototypes, Nos 100, 98 and 171, were clearly influenced by American practice, which was well documented by contemporary engineering journals. If the rugged basic simplicity of the American engines appealed to him, then so did the more sophisticated and refined machinery which was currently appearing in Europe. He resolved to discover, at first hand, the true value of the impressive claims made on behalf of the French De Glehn-Du Bousquet four-cylinder compounds, and obtained authority to purchase three such engines for comparative trials against his own prototypes.

The subsequent performance of the French engines had important effects upon some aspects of Churchward's policy of standardisation. Although, of course, their design is not in any way attributable to him, they are therefore included here as an integral part of the story of Churchward locomotives.

Below: First of the French trio was No 102 *La France,* which was built by the Société Alsacienne des Constructions Méchaniques, Belfort, in 1903 and delivered to Swindon for reassembly (arriving in 13 packing cases) and attachment to a standard 4000-gallon tender. The engine was virtually a replica of Nord Railway of France Nos 2 641/2, apart from GWR items such as the lipped chimney (*not,* however, of recognisably Swindon design), the smokebox door and the brake equipment. The first livery applied was black with red and white lining, as seen here. Boiler pressure was 227lb psi and tractive effort was 23,710lb at 85 per cent. Separate sets of Walschaerts valve gear were provided for the high- and low-pressure cylinders./*Ian Allan Library*

Top right: Nos 103 and 104, which were built two years later (also at Belfort), were similar to the Paris-Orleans Railway 3001 class and were also similar to, but larger than No 102. Like *La France,* in due course, they received names, which had echoes of *L'Entente Cordiale;* No 103 was *President* and 104 was *Alliance.* At about the same time (1907) they received copper-capped GWR-style chimneys. These handsome engines had side-window cabs (reduced to suit the GWR loading gauge) and standard 3500-gallon tenders. When the original boilers required repair they were swapped between locomotives and also alternated with Swindon standard No 1 boilers. The bogie design so impressed Churchward that he adopted it for the GWR, commencing with the Star class 4-6-0s and the Pacific *The Great Bear,* the principal modification being the use of coil springs for the side control as opposed to the swing links of Swindon practice. The Dean suspension bogie was also redesigned on the De Glehn principle for the Flower class and Bird series of Bulldog 4-4-0s./*Ian Allan Library*

Centre right: No 104 *Alliance* seen running with non-superheated long-cone standard No 1 boiler about 1907. New elbowed outside steampipes were a necessity of this rebuilding, foreshadowing a similar application to the Castle class and others in later years. The copper-capped GWR chimney had a capuchon, and both chimney and safety valve bonnet were shorter than usual to clear the loading gauge. The three engines survived over 20 years; in later days they were at Oxford for work on the Paddington-Birmingham line./*Ian Allan Library*

Bottom right: The superheated long-cone Swindon No 1 boiler, with top feed, and the copper-capped chimney with capuchon, produced a rakishly handsome locomotive when applied to No 103 *President.* Perhaps the outside valve motion and side-window cab added up – dare one suggest it – to a more modern appearance than that of contemporary Churchward engines. The boiler carries the standard four-cone ejector, with the pipe running beneath the handrail on the boiler side. The GWR route classification, carried on the cabsides, was B, red./*Ian Allan Library*

The Churchward Standard Locomotives

For ease of reference, the prototype locomotives are included in the section dealing with the production version of each type. These sections are in the chronological order of appearance of each prototype from Swindon, rather than in sequence of wheel arrangement or power class.

The later production of Churchward designed standard locomotives took place under the auspices of C. B. Collett and F. W. Hawksworth, but in view of the relatively minor modifications involved, they are included in this part.

2900 class; 2 cyl 4-6-0 (The Saints) Express Passenger Engines

Introduced: 1902
Total: 77
GWR classification: C, Red
BR Power Class: 4P

The prototype two-cylinder 4-6-0 locomotive, No 100 has already been discussed in the Introduction and it could be argued that this and the next two 4-6-0s, Nos 98 and 171, were only members of the Saint class in later days, when they had been brought into line with new boilers, etc. However, the early Churchward engines were the true genesis of the type and deserve inclusion in this section, although No 100 is illustrated in original form on page 18.

The second locomotive, No 98, may be described as the first true example of the Churchward standard engine, and also the first Saint proper. With a short-cone taper boiler, tapered firebox and 200lb psi pressure, the locomotive also differed considerably from No 100 at the front-end, and set the pattern for future construction. The two cylinders were cast with their half saddles and bolted together, as well as to the bar-type front extension frames. The piston valves were increased to 10in diameter, with a travel of $5\frac{7}{8}$in, which was later increased to the final standard of $6\frac{1}{4}$in. Churchward wished to avoid inclined cylinders, and as the cylinders for the 4-6-0s

Below: The drawing illustrates the latter-day condition of some locomotives, with outside steampipes, superheated boiler with top feed and Holcroft-style framing with curved drop ends.

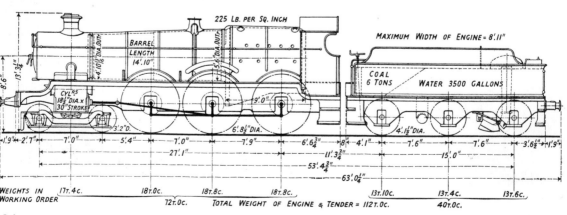

Top: Churchward's second 4-6-0, No 98, which appeared in March 1903, was the true forerunner of his standardisation scheme, with many improvements over No 100 — in particular, the layout of the front end and valve gear. When new the locomotive had a short-cone taper boiler, as illustrated, with 200lb psi pressure, a tube heating surface of 1988.65sq ft and a firebox heating surface of 154.39sq ft, giving a total of 2143.94sq ft. The high running plate and rakish line of the boiler echoed American practice of the period and was a marked breakaway from the heavy double frames of the Dean period. Tractive effort when new was 20,530lb at 85 per cent and a 4000-gallon tender was attached. Later renumbered 2998 and named (first and briefly) *Vanguard,* then *Ernest Cunard.*/*Ian Allan Library*

Above: The third of Churchward's prototype 4-6-0s was No 171 *Albion* (later No 2971), which was basically similar to No 98 except that it had 225lb psi boiler pressure, and was constructed for testing against the French locomotive *La France,* which had 228lb psi pressure (see page 22). The increase in pressure to 225lb became standard, and raised No 171's tractive effort to 23,090lb at 85 per cent. There were slight alterations to firebox heating surface and overall weight. The engine is seen here in new condition, with short-cone taper boiler, at the head of an express near Acton. The nameplate is fitted to the splasher without a distance piece, a feature carried by this particular locomotive throughout its days./*LGRP*

25

26

Top left: As built, *Albion* had about 50 per cent more adhesion than the French Compound by virtue of the 4-6-0 wheel arrangement. To permit a closer comparison to be made, Churchward had No 171 altered to a 4-4-2 by replacing the trailing pair of coupled wheels with a two-wheel truck. This modification lasted from October 1904 to July 1907. In 1905 Churchward was still examining the relative merits of the 4-4-2 and the 4-6-0 wheel arrangement and a further 19 basically similar locomotives were produced, of which 13 were 4-4-2s (Nos 172/9-90) and the rest were 4-6-0s (Nos 173-8). For a few months in 1907 *Albion* was renamed *The Pirate,* afterwards reverting to its original name./*Ian Allan Library*

Centre left: Later named *Winterstoke,* No 176 is seen here in original condition with short-cone taper boiler and short smokebox. The Swindon builder's plate is beneath the smokebox door. The tender was of 3500 gallons compared to the 4000 gallons capacity of No 98, and Nos 173-8 were slightly heavier than No 171 when running as a 4-6-0. A number of these engines ran without nameplates when new It was in this state, without the later additions of brass ornamentation, that the Churchward 4-6-0s looked most like their American contemporaries./*Ian Allan Library*

Bottom left: This second picture of No 176 complete with nameplate shows a number of alterations, in particular the extended smokebox, capuchon chimney and addition of brass beading to the driving wheel splashers. The short-cone taper boiler is retained./*Ian Allan Library*

Below: One of the Atlantics, No 181 *Ivanhoe,* in original condition; and a very pleasing picture it makes, with polished rods and the generally high standard of cleaning which was then the norm. The nameplate has the distance piece and the splashers have brass beading./*Ian Allan Library*

were designed in common with those of the 2-8-0 prototype No 97 (see page 43) he was obliged to raise the cylinder centre line $2\frac{1}{2}$in above the driving wheel axle centres (as otherwise the cylinders would have fouled the loading gauge with worn tyres on the smaller coupled wheels of the 2-8-0). This feature was common to his earlier standard types, but was later abandoned for the larger-wheeled engines.

The third engine, No 171, was basically similar to No 98 except for an increase in boiler pressure to 225lb psi, which raised the tractive effort from 20,530lb to 23,090lb at 85 per cent, and there were slight changes in the firebox design and engine weight. By then Churchward was concerned to prove his new engines against the first of the three De Glehn-Du Bousquet Atlantics, No 102 *La France,* and he accordingly modified No 171 to the 4-4-2 wheel arrangement. During the period of uncertainty which followed he produced further basically identical engines of both 4-4-2 and 4-6-0 wheel arrangement.

By 1906 the die was cast for GWR locomotive policy. Churchward had decided in favour of the 4-6-0 layout because of the greater adhesion available from the six coupled wheels, and he had satisfied himself that the intricacies of compounding were not of superior value to the simple expansion layout for GWR conditions. He therefore proceeded with two versions of the 4-6-0, in order to ascertain the relative merits of two and four cylinders. One was the existing two-

cylinder layout (and eventually involved converting the existing 4-4-2s back to 4-6-0s); the other was the four-cylinder layout of the superb Star class (see section 7 page 64.)

Production of the two-cylinder version, with 10 locomotives Nos 2901-10, started in May 1906 and continued until 1913, during which time steady improvement was made to the boiler design, including provision of superheating and top feed. No 2901 was delivered with a Schmidt firetube superheater, thereby initiating the modern superheated locomotive in this country. A further increase in cylinder diameter to $18\frac{1}{8}$in took place with Nos 2902-10 and in later years it was standardised at $18\frac{1}{2}$in, producing a tractive effort for the class of 24,395lb. Further modifications by Collett and Hawksworth, including the provision of new front ends, added up to the following latter-day dimensions: Total heating surface (evaporative) 1841.38sq ft, comprising a tube heating surface of 1686.60sq ft, a firebox heating surface of 154.78sq ft and a superheated heating surface of 262.62sq ft; and total engine weight of 72 tons. The tender weight varied according to the pattern of tender used in later days (see illustrations).

Above right: At the end of December 1912, the running numbers of the early locomotives, Nos 100, 171-90 and 98, became 2900/71-90/8, thus coming into line with the Ladies and Saints. The Ladies, Nos 2901-10, had all been delivered in May 1906 but differed in that Nos 2904/5/6 had short-cone boilers and short smokeboxes while Nos 2902/3/7-10 had long-cone boilers with medium extension to the smokeboxes. No 2901 *Lady Superior* was built with a Schmidt superheater (the first modern superheater locomotive to run in Britain) and Nos 2902-10 had $18\frac{1}{8}$in diameter cylinders, which raised their tractive effort to 23,382lb at 85 per cent. The superheated engine ran with boiler pressure reduced to 200lb and an increased cylinder diameter of $18\frac{3}{4}$in, thereby reducing tractive effort to 21,457lb. No 2910 *Lady of Shalott* is seen at Hereford in later condition with a long-cone Swindon superheated boiler, with top feed, extended smokebox and chimney capuchon./*Ian Allan Library*

Right: The Saints followed the Ladies in 1908, and were numbered 2911-30. As built these had long-cone non-superheated boilers and smokeboxes of medium length. They retained the smaller pattern chimney, with capuchon added. Perhaps the most striking feature had nothing to do with their performance. It was the redesign by Holcroft, to Churchward's direction, of the framing, to improve the appearance of the engines and this is clearly evident if comparison is made with the view of No 171 taken at the same location (page 25). The engines had screw reverse fitted. In their original state, with an absence of exterior fittings these locomotives were undeniably handsome and a nice touch was the location of the Swindon works plate on the centre splasher. Superheating of the entire class began in earnest in 1909 and was completed by 1912. Top feed apparatus (see preceding picture of No 2910) made its appearance in 1911, with No 2917 carrying an early separate version. No 2917 is seen here prior to this application; it was named *Saint Bernard*./*The Cecil J. Allen Collection*

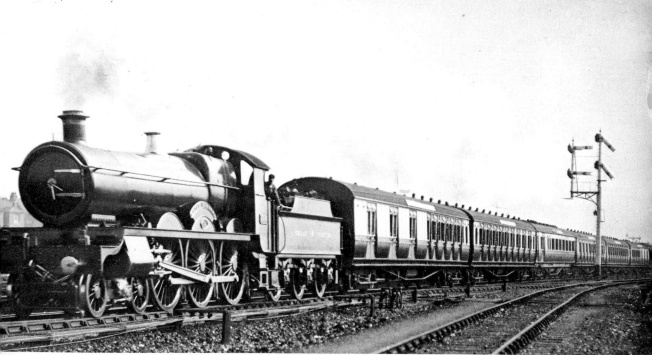

For high-speed express working Churchward opted for the four-cylinder Star layout, leaving the two-cylinder Saints as more general-purpose machines; in so doing he set a pattern which was to be widely imitated elsewhere during the next 50 years, producing such notable engines as Collett's Hall, Stanier's Black Fives and Thompson's B1 as well as the final BR standard engines — all of which belong to the Saint class family tree.

When new, the Saints were to be seen on the West of England main line, later extending their activities to areas such as Wolverhampton and West Wales, and later still to South Wales. No 2915 had the distinction of working the inaugural Cheltenham Flyer and Saints headed this train frequently. Examples of the class achieved a mileage of approximately two million before withdrawal. When the GWR handed over its locomotive stock to British Railways in 1948 there were 47 survivors; all had gone by 1953.

The engines were built as follows:

No 100 (2900)	Swindon	1902
No 98 (2998)	Swindon	1903

Left: Churchward's original 4-6-0 No 100 was renumbered 2900, to become the first of the 2900 class, or Saints. It was, however, unique in the design of the framing, cylinders and valve gear. Various re-boilerings took place, and the locomotive is seen here with a superheated long-cone boiler with top feed, tall safety valve bonnet, four cone ejector, large-diameter chimney and extended smokebox. The bogie brakes have been removed. Another feature unique to *William Dean* was the solid backplate to the cab footsteps, which were slotted on all other Churchward engines. The non-standard cylinders (which necessitated the extra depth to front-end framing and bufferbeam) were worn out by mid-1932, and this remarkable locomotive was then condemned after 30 years service. Its latter-day condition, as illustrated here, makes a fascinating comparison to the picture on page 18./*Ian Allan Library*

Below left: Nos 2931-55 were constructed between 1911-13 and were named Courts. They were built new with superheaters, top feed and extended smokebox (although some of the boilers were secondhand) and they had the revised framing style of the Saints. It is worthwhile mentioning that this framing style was applied also to the 4-4-2s when rebuilt as 4-6-0s between April 1912 and January 1913. The Courts had the cylinder centre line coincident with that of the coupled wheels, whereas the earlier engines had the cylinder centre line $2\frac{1}{2}$in above that of the driving wheel centres. Commencing with No 2941, the cylinder diameter was increased to $18\frac{1}{2}$in, which became standard for the whole class in due course, raising the tractive effort to

24,395lb. No 2946 *Langford Court* is seen in later condition, with small casing to the safety valves (introduced in 1927) and shield to the whistles (introduced in 1925), with the standard GWR audible signalling (ATC) equipment below the buffer beam, and later 3500-gallon tender, with continuous fender. Note the absence of bogie brakes, a feature removed from earlier locomotives by Collett./*Ian Allan Library*

Below: Under Collett two engines of the class received substantial alterations. One was No 2925 *Saint Martin,* which was rebuilt as prototype of the Hall class*, the other was No 2935 *Caynham Court* which was modified in 1932 with rotary cam poppet valve gear and new cylinders. The only poppet valve engine on the GWR, it was one of the few departures from the standard Churchward practice in valve gear. The locomotive is seen here, on shed at Swindon, August 16, 1936, with 3500-gallon long-fendered tender and with the upper lamp bracket moved to the smokebox door (a feature introduced from 1932 onward)./*H. C. Casserley*

*See Appendix 1.

No 171 (2971)	Swindon	1903
Nos 172-180 (2972-2980)	Swindon	1905
Nos 181-190 (2981-2990)	Swindon	1905
Nos 2901-2910	Swindon	1906
Nos 2911-2930	Swindon	1907
Nos 2931-2940	Swindon	1911
Nos 2941-2950	Swindon	1912
Nos 2951-2955	Swindon	1913

Two engines of the class, Nos 2925 *Saint Martin* and 2935 *Caynham Court,* were modified by Collett. The more extensive rebuilding was applied to No 2925 in 1924, when this engine was reconstructed as the prototype for his famous Hall class (see Appendix 1). The other engine was given rotary cam poppet valve gear and new cylinders, but was still counted as a Saint.

First of class withdrawn: 2985 (1931)
Last of class withdrawn: 2920 (1953)
None preserved.

Top left: Another view of No 2935 *Caynham Court,* this time with the locomotive attached to a 4000 gallon tender and seen at the head of a down Cheltenham express in Sonning Cutting. A number of modifications were made to the valve gear during the life of the locomotive, but it was apparently not considered worthwhile extending the application, which incidentally added about two tons in weight to the engine./M. W. Earley

Centre left: Also seen in Sonning Cutting, working a down semi-fast, is No 2971 (originally 171) *Albion* (see also page 25). Despite the addition of a superheated top-feed boiler and large-diameter chimney, the engine retains the tall safety valve bonnet and original nameplates, without distance piece to splasher, and has the original Churchward framing with square drop-ends and three footsteps to the cab. Minor modifications include lowered top lamp bracket, provision of whistle shield and long-fender version of the 3500-gallon tender./M. W. Earley

Bottom left: Nos 2902/3/5/6/8 had the front end altered from the square Churchward pattern to the curved Holcroft style, but retained the original layout of cab and three footsteps at the rear end. This occurred when they were fitted with new cylinders, outside steampipes and new extension frames, modifications intended to give the engines a further lease of life of about 25 years. No 2906 is seen here in rebuilt form, at the head of a local westbound freight at Leckwith Junction, Cardiff on July 26, 1952. *Lady of Lynn* still presents a powerful appearance after approximately 46 years in service, but it was destined for withdrawal just one month later. The outside steampipes were fitted in October 1935./R. C. Riley

Below: The LNWR-style lined-black mixed-traffic livery of early British Railways days sits rather uneasily on No 2937 *Clevedon Court.* The engine had recently received outside steampipes and was attached to a 4000-gallon tender, showing the final appearance of those examples of the class which survived nationalisation; this engine lasted until 1953. The brass beading to the driving wheel splashers was removed from the class as part of World War I austerity measures and was not subsequently replaced, although in this instance the Swindon painters have enlarged the lining out on the splashers to simulate beading. The numberplates and nameplates had red backgrounds at the time. The four-cone – or torpedo-ejector, is visible, fitted to the right-hand side of the firebox, with its pipe running behind the handrail for the length of the boiler and entering the smokebox at a point beneath the chimney. Churchward began fitting this powerful type of ejector to his larger locomotives – both passenger and mixed-traffic types – in 1913, including the Stars, the three French Compounds and the 4-6-2 *The Great Bear./Ian Allan Library*

2800 class; 2 cyl 2-8-0 Heavy Freight Engines

Introduced: 1903
Total: 168
GWR Classification: E, Blue
BR Power Class: 8F

Although Churchward is often, justifiably, acclaimed for producing the country's first Pacific design (*The Great Bear* of 1908,) it is not so widely realised that he introduced an equally noteworthy innovation to British practice five years earlier, when the first 2-8-0 appeared. It was the prototype No 97 (later No 2800), which came out in June 1903. The engine was conceived alongside his prototype 4-6-0 two-cylinder engine No 98 (see page 24) and had many of the improvements that were also featured in that locomotive. Intended for mineral traffic, the 2-8-0 had 4ft $7\frac{1}{2}$in coupled wheels and the same boiler type as the 4-6-0.

When new, the dimensions of No 97 were as follows: Cylinders 18in stroke by 30in diameter; saturated steam boiler with a total heating surface of 2143.04sq ft, consisting of a tube heating surface of 1988.65sq ft and a firebox heating surface of 154.39sq ft; boiler pressure of 200lb (later raised to 225lb); and tractive effort of 29,775lb at 85 per cent.

Below: The drawing illustrates the 2800 class after the addition of top feed and superheating, and with the curved front drop ends introduced with Nos 2831-5 of 1911.

Top right: Churchward's prototype 2-8-0 heavy freight locomotive, No 97, came out in June 1903. Although photographed in works grey equivalent of the standard lined-green livery, the engine was actually finished in an experimental livery of black with red lining. This was the first 2-8-0 in the country and the prototype of a class destined to survive until the final days of WR steam operation. The main difference between No 97 and her production followers was in the lower pitch of the boiler (at 7ft $5\frac{1}{2}$in), which also had the barrel clothing in five sections instead of the later four. The short-cone boiler had a pressure of 200lb. The tender was an early 4000-gallon design, of which about 20 were built between 1901 and 1904./*British Rail*

Centre right: No 2803 of the first production batch of standard Consolidation goods engines, Nos 2801-20, which came out in 1905, with Churchward's standardisation policy under way. Obvious difference was the daylight visible below the boiler, which was pitched at 8ft 2in and had 225lb pressure. (No 97 was subsequently altered to match.) The chimney was originally of the small-diameter pattern shown here, and on No 97, but the tender was a lighter 3000-gallon design./*Collection: A. Swain*

Bottom right: Boiler improvements were effected steadily on subsequent batches of the 2-8-0s, both long-cone and short-cone versions were carried, and changed around. The smokebox was extended to medium and then full length, and superheaters were added from March 1909 (No 2808 being the first one). A larger chimney was used, and starting with Nos 2831-5 of 1911, the front end was refashioned with curved drop ends. Strengthening struts were added between the saddle and the buffer beam. A 3500-gallon tender (with longer side fenders) became general for the class. Top feed was added from 1911 and from 1915 the trailing sandboxes altered in design, to be filled from below the running plate. No 2844 is seen with most of the foregoing alterations, plus a cast-iron chimney of similar dimensions to the standard copper cap. The cab roof has a gutter strip added. The top lamp bracket is placed on the smokebox top and the vacuum brake swan neck rises well above the buffer beam./*Ian Allan Library*

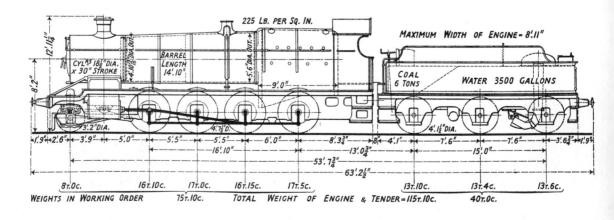

The first production locomotives appeared in 1905. Compared to No 97 they had boilers pitched $8\frac{1}{2}$in higher, 225lb boiler pressure, 3000 gallon (instead of 4000) tenders, and piston valves increased from $8\frac{1}{2}$in to 10in diameter. The total engine weight remained at 68 tons 6cwt, but the weights were more evenly distributed, and the smaller tender weighed 36 tons 15 cwt instead of the 43 tons 3 cwt of the 4000 gallon version. Total weight of engine and tender was reduced to 105 tons 1 cwt. Tractive effort was 33,495lb. The engines were numbered 2801-20.

The next batch to appear, Nos 2821-30 of 1907, had the cylinder diameter increased to $18\frac{3}{8}$in, thereby increasing the tractive effort still further to 34,905lb. Superheating followed in 1909 (No 2808 was the first fitted) and yet another increase in cylinder diameter to $18\frac{1}{2}$in, finalised the tractive effort for the class at 35,380lb. With long-cone boilers and extended smokeboxes, plus superheating, the total heating surface was 1873.12sq ft, with the tubes providing 1608.14sq ft, the firebox 150.37sq ft, and the superheater 264.98 sq ft. Further modifications to the superheated surface took place over the years.

Below: The narrower cast-iron chimney carried by No 2847 when this picture was taken, plus the addition of outside steampipes to the cylinders, are noticeable changes. Outside steampipes were fitted from 1934 onwards to all but a few of the class. The engine is fitted with ATC (with conduit visible along the running plate) and has lost the gutter strip on the cab roof. The vacuum brake swan neck has been lowered, but the engine retains the tall safety valve bonnet and lamp bracket on the smokebox top. This view clearly showed the daylight between boiler and frames which was a distinctive feature of the class./*M. W. Earley*

Right: No less than 20 years elapsed between delivery of the final engine, No 2883, of the 84 locomotives built during Churchward's regime (in 1919) and the beginnings of further new construction by Collett. Nos 2884-99 and 3800-66 appeared between 1938 and 1942. Known as the 2884 class, they were an updated version of Churchward's basic standard design. Modifications included side-window cabs, outside steam pipes, short safety valve bonnets, provision of whistle shield and (most noticeable in this view) the provision of a fire-iron casing on the left-hand side ahead of the cab. No 3832 was photographed at Oxford on April 24, 1962./*R. S. Greenwood*

Below right: Between 1945 and 1947 12 of the 2800 and 8 of the later version were equipped for oil burning, as part of a government-inspired plan, abandoned in 1948. It increased their weight (mainly the tender) and involved some renumbering. No 4857 (original No 3831) was converted in August 1947 and ran as an oil burner until May 1949 in the condition shown here. The 4850 (ex-2884) class conversions had sliding shutters outside the cab windows. The filler nozzle for the oil fuel can be seen between the rear two wheels of the tender./*P. Ransome-Wallis*

Alterations to improve weight distribution, by means of the addition of heavy castings to the frames were introduced with No 2846 (altered in 1917) and were also a feature of Nos 2856 onwards, as built. Outside steampipes requiring new front ends were fitted to these locomotives from 1934 and improvements were made to the framing, in most cases, giving them curved front drop ends in place of the original Churchward square treatment.

Perhaps the soundness of the design lay in its basic simplicity and fitness for the job; certainly it proved unnecessary for Collett to make any great alterations before he produced a further batch of engines 20 years later, when the 2884 class appeared. These were numbered 2884-3866 and were built between 1938 and 1942. They were slightly heavier than previous engines, at 76 tons 5 cwt, and had updated features such as side-window cabs, outside steam pipes and modified framing and motion bracket. The side

Above: No greater tribute to Churchward exists than the selection of a design originating in 1903 for participation in the 1948 Locomotives Exchanges organised by the newly formed Railway Executive. The Exchange trials were to assist in preparing designs for the new range of BR standard steam locomotives then under consideration. No 3803, of the 2884 series, was photographed leaving Acton Yard on the 11.20am freight for South Wales on August 12, 1948, with the LNER dynamometer car next to the tender, during the course of the Exchange trials./*C. C. B. Herbert*

Above right: No 2881, photographed in BR black livery, with the short-version safety valve bonnet and top lamp bracket lowered to smokebox door. The class was not often employed on passenger turns, but was sometimes a prize for the photographer, as here, when the engine was caught leaving Torquay with the Saturday 9.05am Kingswear-Cardiff train on September 3, 1955./*Peter W. Gray*

Right: In spotless BR black livery, No 2851 makes a superb picture at the head of a train of empties. This class always seemed to carry the plain black extremely well, unlike many Swindon engines./*R. J. Blenkinsop*

windows were not put into the cabs of Nos 3814-66 until after World War II. It was intended to build further examples of the class for overseas war service, but the order was cancelled with the defeat of the BEF in France in 1940, and when further 2-8-0s were built at Swindon they were of the LMS Stanier design then favoured for military use.

The post war Government-sponsored scheme to convert locomotives to oil firing resulted in adaptation of 20 engines before this abortive scheme was dropped. Initially, 10 of the converted engines ran with their original numbers, then late in 1946 the earlier 2800 examples were separated from the later 2884 class. The 2800 oil-burners became 4800-4811 and the 2884 oil-burners became 4850-4857. The sequence of numbers in the order of conversion was, as follows:

Above: The prototype, No 97, was renumbered 2800 in December 1912. Comparison with the picture on page 35 clearly shows the evolution of the design over the years. This picture of No 2800 was taken at Swindon in 1953, with the engine in ex-works condition, at a late stage in her career (withdrawal came only five years later). The entire front-end design had altered over the span of half a century, and the engine had new cylinders, outside steampipes, fully extended smokebox, and curved drop ends ahead of the cylinders, plus many minor detail alterations./*G. Wheeler*

Right: No 3864 was one of the final engines built, in November 1942, and remained virtually unaltered in detail for its entire career, being withdrawn in July 1965. /*N. E. Preedy*

Original No.	New No.	Original No.	New No.
3837	4854	3820	4856
3813	4855	3831	4857

The first engine was converted in September 1948 (No 2872) and the last to run as an oil-burner was No 4808 (ex 2834,) reconverted to coal in January 1950.

Heavy coal traffic was the original duty the 2800 class was called upon to work, but they gradually extended both their sphere of operation and their range of duties, until in final post-war days they were even to be found on local goods workings. A feature of the class operationally was its tendency to be absent from home shed for lengthy periods; in order to keep a check on boiler wash-out dates,

Original No.	New No.	Original No.	New No.
2872*	4800	2834	4808
2854*	4801	2845	4809
2862*	4802	2853	4810
2849*	4803	2847	4811
2839*	4804	2888*	4850
2863*	4805	3865*	4851
2832*	4806	3818*	4852
2848	4807	3839	4853

*Ran at first with original numbers whilst oil-burners.

therefore, each engine carried a report card in a small container welded to the footplate valance above the left-hand cylinder.

The engines were built as follows:

No 97 (2800)	Swindon	1903
Nos 2801-2810	Swindon	1905
Nos 2811-2820	Swindon	1905
Nos 2821-2830	Swindon	1907
Nos 2831-2835	Swindon	1911
Nos 2836-2845	Swindon	1912
Nos 2846-2855	Swindon	1912-13
Nos 2856-2883	Swindon	1918-19
Nos 2884-2899	Swindon	1938-39
Nos 3800-3803	Swindon	1938-39
Nos 3804-3823	Swindon	1939-40
Nos 3824-3833	Swindon	1940-41
Nos 3834-3843	Swindon	1941-42
Nos 3844-3866	Swindon	1942

In January 1921, No 2804 visited Scotland for trials on the Glenfarg incline of the North British Railway, during which it hauled a train of 590 tons up an average gradient of 1 in 75 for $6\frac{3}{4}$ miles.

First of class withdrawn: 2800 (1958)
Last of class withdrawn: 3836 (1965)
Examples preserved: 2818, 2857

3100 (later 5100), 3150, 5101, 6100, 8100, 3100 (of 1938) Classes
2-6-2T
Passenger Tank Engines

Introduced : 1903
Total : 306*
GWR Classification : 3100 D, Red
then (as 5100) D, Blue
5101 D, Blue
6100 D, Blue
8100 D, Blue
3100 D, Red.
BR Power Class : 4MT

The prototype for this large series of 2-6-2T engines, No 99, appeared in 1903 and was subjected to the typical Churchward proving period before the type was multiplied. The initial production batch, built in 1905-06, set the standards for a class which was steadily increased in numbers over the years, the last batch being constructed in the early days of nationalisation.

The total given comprises the following: 3100 (40); 3150 (41); 5101 (140); 6100 (70); 8100 (10) and 3100 of 1938 (5).

As built, No 99 had the typical cylinder dimensions of 18in diameter by 30in stroke and coupled wheels of 5ft 8in. The boiler was pressed for 195lb psi and the total heating surface was 1517.89sq ft, with the tube heating surface 1396.58sq ft and the firebox heating surface 121.31sq ft. The tractive effort was 23,690lb at 85 per cent, and with a water tank capacity of 1380 gallons the engine weighed 72 tons 3cwt in working order. The spring gear was equalised throughout.

As the class was subsequently sub-divided into batches, with detail differences, each series is dealt with under the appropriate heading.

Right: No 99, the prototype of the large 2-6-2Ts, appeared in 1903 and was thoroughly tried and tested by Churchward before more locomotives were built, with detail differences, in 1905-6. As portrayed, No 99 is in original condition with a short cone taper boiler, slender cast-iron chimney and short straight-topped side tanks. It received a long-cone boiler in 1910 but the side tanks were not altered until April 1929, when the engine was finally renumbered 5100. (It had an interim number change to 3100 in December 1912). Features to note include the provision of a padlocked toolbox above the cylinder and the location of the single maker's plate below the smokebox door. No monogram or company crest was carried — but of course the locomotive was *obviously* Great Western! The cab sides were set inwards above the tank and bunker./*Ian Allan Library*

Below right: After two years a further 39 engines, Nos 3111-3149, appeared in 1905/6. They had larger tanks, with sloping top at the forward end, and the cab sides were flush. The same slender cast-iron chimney was applied to the short smokebox. Long-cone boilers were fitted and, in common with No 99, Nos 3111-29 had the steam brake and double pull rods, but Nos 3130 onwards were vacuum braked, although this picture of No 3120 shows no evidence of the outside pull rods, which might have been added later./*Collection A. Swain*

Below: The drawing shows the 3100 class as renumbered in the 5100 series, with altered weight distribution and extended bunkers.

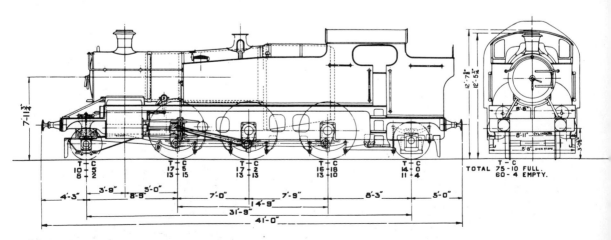

3100 series (later 5100)

The first of these appeared after No 99 had been on trial for over a year. They differed in having larger tanks which held 2000 gallons, thereby increasing the weight to 75 tons 10cwt. In 1919 the tractive effort was increased to 24,300lb when the boiler pressure was standardised at 200lb. In the period 1919-22 coal capacity was increased by approximately 18cwt by means of a bunker extension. Weight distribution problems arose and for a while Nos 3112-8/20 ran with the tank capacity reduced to 1600 gallons. Modifications to improve weight distribution allowed a return to the original tank capacity and, after alteration the whole class was renumbered in the 5100 series, capable of running over the D blue routes.

The engines were built as follows:

No 99 (3100) later 5100   Swindon 1903
Nos 3111-3120 (5111-5120) Swindon 1905
Nos 3121-3130 (5121-5130) Swindon 1905
Nos 3131-3149 (5131-5149) Swindon 1906

First of class withdrawn*: 5127, 5146 (1948)
Last of class withdrawn: 5148 (1959)
None preserved.

*Not including Nos 5115/6/8/20/3/4/6/33/45 and 5100, withdrawn in 1937-39 and rebuilt as 8100 class (see page 52)

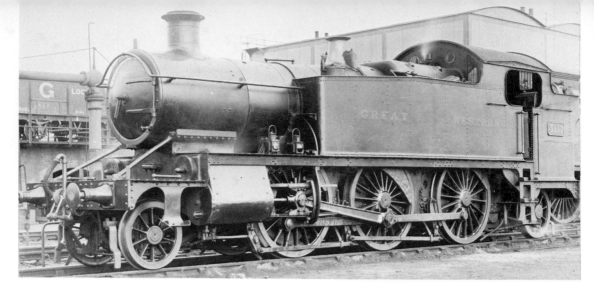

Top left: No 3117, built in 1905, is seen here in later condition, with the front end struts between smokebox and bufferbeam, which were added in 1909 as heavy work such as banking had resulted in weakened or buckled front end frames. In this picture the outside set of the double pull rods for the steam brake can be clearly seen. Evidently there were weight distribution problems with these locomotives, which finally led to modifications in 1928-30 and a general renumbering. The alterations were:

When running as 3100: 9 tons × 17 tons 13 × 18 tons 4 × 18 tons 4 × 12 tons 9.
Renumbered as 5100: 10 tons 5 × 17 tons 5 × 17 tons 2 × 16 tons 18 × 14 tons.

Other items of note are the large diameter chimney, introduced 1908-10, the removal of the toolbox, the removal of the works plate, the addition of top feed and superheating and the enlarged coal bunker at the rear end (undertaken between 1919-22) with the numberplate moved from the tankside. A small step has been added ahead of the cylinders./*Ian Allan Library*

Centre left: One of the vacuum-braked engines, No 3133 built in 1906, seen in later condition with taped cast-iron chimney and top feed on the superheated boiler. The small dome-shaped cover on the footplate below the smokebox housed the pony truck springing. The original Churchward cab is still carried, complete with the two circular porthole windows above the firebox; these were later blanked-off and the engines received new cab roofs (except one or two) from 1931 onward. The renumbering of Nos 3100 (ex 99), 3111-3149 to Nos 5100, 5111-49 took place between 1928-30./*Ian Allan Library*

Below left: No 3131 showing the extended bunker capacity with raised fender at the rear; modified cab roof; and porthole spectacle plates removed. A smaller safety valve bonnet and smaller large diameter chimney have been fitted. The bunker design was altered again in the 1930s, mostly at the rear end with the provision of recessed fenders, and sliding shutters were added to the cab sides. The original 2-6-2Ts had the square drop ends to the framing of early Churchward practice, but in about 1943 some had new curved front ends and outside steam pipes fitted./*Ian Allan Library*

Below: The last of the 3100 series, No 3150 appeared in 1906 but with the larger standard No 4 boiler, and became in fact the first of a new 3150 class, as the experiment was obviously a success. The usual Churchward trial period, in this case of a

3150 series

By placing a standard No 4 boiler on the last of the 3100 batch, in 1906, Churchward created the larger and more powerful 3150 class. No 3150 differed from the production engines that followed, in having 18in-diameter cylinders instead of $18\frac{1}{2}$in, producing a tractive effort of 24,300lb. The 40 subsequent engines had a tractive effort of 25,670lb. The No 4 boiler had a tube heating surface of 1692.14sq ft and a firebox heating surface of 128.21sq ft, giving a total of 1820.35sq ft. The grate area was 20.56sq ft and boiler pressure was 200lb. Wheel diameter and wheelbase were the same as for the 3100 series, but the full working weight was increased to 78 tons 16cwt, with a tank capacity of 2000 gallons. The engines were used mostly for banking duties and it was the strain caused by this upon the front end frames which led Churchward to introduce the struts, which later became standard for his other classes fitted with leading pony trucks.

The class is perhaps best remembered in service on pilot duties through the Severn Tunnel, although in addition to the banking

year, elapsed before any further locomotives were built. No 3160 portrayed here was built in 1907 and was the first to receive the front struts. What impressive engines they were for the period, with the high-pitched taper boiler surmounted by a tall polished safety valve bonnet. The engine has the original slender cast-iron chimney and large works plate below the smokebox. It is seen at Platform 6 in Paddington Station, with a good head of steam ready for departure. When new, Nos 3166-70 had two-way water pick-up apparatus, which lasted for about four years./*Ian Allan Library*

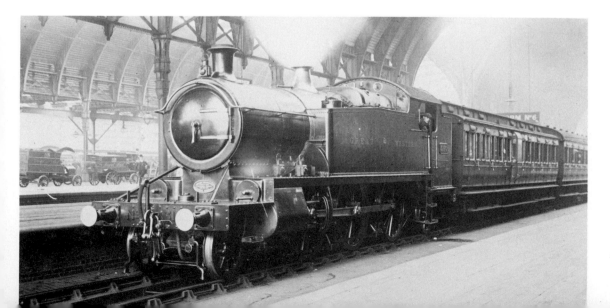

Top left: By the time this picture of No 3156 was taken a substantial change in appearance had evolved through Churchward's progressive policies of improvement — a policy also carried on by his successor C. B. Collett. The locomotive has a superheated boiler with top feed (but retains the tall safety valve bonnet), a large-diameter chimney and enlarged and extended bunker./*Ian Allan Library*

Centre left: 3100 2-6-2T No 3164 piloting Castle class 4-6-0 No 7006 *Lydford Castle*, on the climb to Sapperton Tunnel, with the 11.35 Cheltenham, Gloucester and Paddington in March 1951, photographed at Frampton Crossing, near Chalford, with the gradient at 1 in 60. The tank engine has been rebuilt at the front end, with outside steam pipes and curved framing (this was the first of the class to receive them in 1934). Nos 3154/7/86 had outside steam pipes retaining the square drop-ends (3186 later received the curved type). The upper lamp bracket is shown in the later position on the smokebox door, and the engine has sliding cab side shutters./*P. M. Alexander*

Bottom left: Another view of No 3164 hard at work, this time banking a freight up the hill to Sapperton Tunnel, March 3, 1953, showing the fender at the rear of the bunker which was recessed to take the upper lamp bracket. A scheme to rebuild the whole 3150 class as smaller-wheeled banking engines (new 3100 series) was curtailed by the outbreak of the 1939-45 war, only five were actually rebuilt and a sixth, No 3170, was returned to stock unaltered./*G. F. Heiron*

work already mentioned they were employed on passenger turns. A scheme to rebuild them as the new 3100 series (see page 52) was halted after only five engines had been dealt with, and their gradual withdrawal started in 1947.

The engines were built as follows:

No 3150	Swindon	1906
Nos 3151-3170	Swindon	1907
Nos 3171-3190	Swindon	1907-08

First of class withdrawn*: 3152, 3162, 3166 (1947)
Last of class withdrawn: 3170 (1958)
None preserved

*Not including Nos 3155/6/73/79/81 withdrawn for rebuilding as 3100-3104 in 1938-39 (See page 52).

Above: Churchward had retired at the end of 1921 to be replaced by C. B. Collett and the emergence of further 2-6-2Ts of Churchward design about eight years later speaks well for the general soundness of the original concept. Collett made only minor changes, to update the class, and construction continued until 1949. First to emerge was No 5101, a revised version of the 5100 (ex 3100) class which became the 5101 series. They had curved drop ends to the framing and outside steampipes. The cab roof was lower and formed of one piece, curved with the sides. An enlarged coal bunker, with recessed rear fender, held four tons of coal. No 5105 is illustrated in works grey finish (for photographic purposes) with copper-cap chimney and tall safety valve bonnet./*Ian Allan Library*

5101 Series

Over 20 years elapsed before any further 2-6-2Ts were built, in 1929-30, and these were an up-dated version of the original 3100 series, called the 5101 class. There was no alteration to the frame length or main dimensions compared with the 1905 Churchward locomotives and the differences were mainly of a detail nature, such as the use of curved drop-ends and a lower cab roof. The bunker held 4 tons and the tank capacity was 2000 gallons. In full working order the total engine weight was 78tons 9cwt. Fitted with superheated boilers,

with top feed, the total heating surface was 1348.95sq ft, consisting of a tube heating surface of 1144.95sq ft a firebox heating surface of 121.80sq ft and a superheater of 82.20sq ft. The grate area remained the same at 20.35sq ft, and boiler pressure was the standard 200lb psi. The class was constructed in batches up to 1949, and the last batch, Nos 4160-4179, had a new superheater arrangement which gave a total heating surface of 1232sq ft.

The operation of this numerous class was over an extremely wide area, with the notable exception of the London suburban area; in the main they were used on passenger work, though some were banking engines, ending their days on pick-up freights after displacement by the BR diesel multiple-units.

The engines were built as follows:

Nos 5101-5110	Swindon	1929-30
Nos 5150-5159	Swindon	1929-30
Nos 5160-5189	Swindon	1930-31
Nos 5190-5199	Swindon	1934
Nos 4100-4119	Swindon	1935-36
Nos 4120-4129	Swindon	1937-38
Nos 4130-4139	Swindon	1939
Nos 4140-4149	Swindon	1946
Nos 4150-4159	Swindon	1947
Nos 4160-4179	Swindon	1948-49

The final series, Nos 4160-4179, never carried GWR livery, although the first six were painted unlined green and lettered BRITISH RAILWAYS in GWR style Egyptian-serif shaded capitals. Nos 4166 onwards first appeared in BR mixed-traffic lined black.

First of class withdrawn: 5159 (1956)
Last of class withdrawn: 4113, 4161 (1965)*
Examples Preserved: 4110, 4141, 4144, 4150, 5164, 5196.

*No 4176 survived in use as a stationary boiler until May 1967, having been withdrawn in October 1965.

Top left: Nos 5101-10/50-9 were built in 1929-30 and were followed by Nos 5160-99 in the period 1930-1934. No 5150 is seen here in British Railways plain black livery, with large totem on tanksides, but proudly sporting a polished copper-cap chimney, leaving Dainton Tunnel with an Exeter-Plymouth local on August 4, 1956. The engine has the squat safety valve cover of later days. Nos 5101-10 had the fender at the rear of the bunker recessed. On Nos 5150 onwards the recess was extended down to include the upper half of the bunker at the rear./*R. J. Blenkinsop*

Above left: The 5101 class was continued in the 4100 series, with the construction of Nos 4100-79 between 1935 and 1949 – thus extending construction of basically Churchward engines into the era of Nationalisation! No 4133 is seen outside Swindon works with a glossy new coat of BR black, devoid of lining, but with a polished copper chimney cap. The sliding shutters to the cabside were applied from new to Nos 5190 onwards, and earlier engines received them during 1930-1./*B. E. Morrison*

Above: Restoration of fully lined out green livery in the later days of the engines' careers (1957 onward) certainly enhanced their appearance. No 4134 was the second tank to be so painted and is seen here at Swindon on February 26, 1957. A late modification can be seen in the three footsteps on the bunker side a feature introduced in 1952 and extended to the greater majority of locomotives remaining in service./*G. Wheeler*

6100 Series

The London area suburban services were improved by the delivery of the 6100 class 2-6-2Ts in the period 1931-35. They were basically similar to the 5101 class except for an increase in boiler pressure to 225lb psi which increased their tractive effort. They were to monopolise the London Division suburban services for about 20 years, only being dispersed after the mid 1950s. Like the 5101 class, they were made redundant by the diesel multiple-units and finished their days on a variety of lesser duties.

The engines were built as follows:

Nos 6100-6129	Swindon	1931
Nos 6130-6159	Swindon	1932-33
Nos 6160-6169	Swindon	1935

First of class withdrawn: 6100 (1958)
Last of class withdrawn: 6111, 6126, 6134/5/ 6, 6141, 6145, 6147, 6156, (1965)
Example preserved: 6160

Top: Constructed specifically for an accelerated London suburban service in the early 1930s the 6100 series were basically similar to the 5101 class but with increased boiler pressure of 225lb psi and an increased tractive effort of 27,340lb. A total of 70 locomotives was delivered between 1931 and 1935. For work over the electrified lines in the London area they were all fitted with LT trip gear for automatic brake application if a signal at danger was inadvertently passed. The standard GWR automatic train control (ATC) gear was arranged to clip up automatically when travelling over electrified sections. No 6113 is seen approaching Old Oak Common on the down line./*E. R. Wethersett*

Above: Seen working a Paddington to High Wycombe train near Gerrards Cross is 6100 class 2-6-2T No 6126. The engine is in an early hybrid British Railways livery, with lettering in GWR serif-Egyptian style and with a small W painted below the numberplates on the bunker sides. This bunker-first view shows the recess at the top of the bunker end, including the fender, to accommodate the lamp bracket. No 6116 was experimentally fitted with smaller wheels in 1932, as follows: pony 3ft, coupled 5ft 3in, and rear radial 3ft 6in, with an increase in tractive effort to 29,510lb. This was to improve acceleration and was part of schemes under consideration by Collett for a new High Acceleration Tank Engine./*C. R. L. Coles*

Top right: Although No 6169 carries a new BR smokebox numberplate in this photograph, taken at Westbourne Park on November 3, 1949, the letters GWR are retained on the tanksides. As the smokebox and chimney have a new coat of black paint it is probable that the engine had received a light repair at its home depot, Southall, in the course of which the numberplate was attached. The low-roof close-coupled suburban carriages are dwarfed by the engine./*W. Gilburt*

Centre right: Resplendent in the lined green livery re-introduced to the Western Region for a number of classes in 1957, No 6167 leaves Paddington working bunker first on a Slough local on April 24, 1957. A feature sometimes felt by passengers travelling behind these locomotives was a gentle fore-and-aft surging motion, transmitted from locomotives to leading carriages through the drawgear. By 1960 new diesel multiple-units were arriving in the London area, rendering these handsome and efficient locomotives redundant./*A. R. Butcher*

Bottom right: Working out its days, No 6155 is seen approaching Norton Junction, near Worcester with a local freight from Evesham – a far cry from the London suburban duties for which it was designed. Photographed on September 19, 1964, just over a year before withdrawal. The three steps welded to the side of the bunker are clearly visible./*K. C. Farmer*

8100 series

A scheme to rebuild withdrawn 5100 class engines, with the new front ends and new boilers of higher pressure, and with smaller coupled wheels, for improved acceleration was suspended by the outbreak of the 1939-45 war. Only 10 locomotives were dealt with, and they had all the improved details of the 5101 series. The higher boiler pressure, of 225lb, meant that they were basically similar to the 6100 series except for the coupled wheel diameter, which was 5ft 6in. Tractive effort was increased to 28,165lb at 85 per cent. It is interesting to note that one of the 10 conversions was the engine which started life as prototype No 99 in 1903 and subsequently became No 3100 (later 5100.) The 10 engines were shedded at various places over the years, ranging from Birmingham to Carmarthen, where their duties included the Pembroke Coast Express.

The engines were rebuilt as follows:

No 8100 (frames ex 5100) Swindon 1938
No 8101 (frames ex 5123) Swindon 1938
No 8102 (frames ex 5118) Swindon 1938
No 8103 (frames ex 5145) Swindon 1938
No 8104 (frames ex 5124) Swindon 1939
No 8105 (frames ex 5126) Swindon 1939
No 8106 (frames ex 5120) Swindon 1939
No 8107 (frames ex 5116) Swindon 1939
No 8108 (frames ex 5133) Swindon 1939
No 8109 (frames ex 5115) Swindon 1939
First of class withdrawn: 8107 (1962)
Last of class withdrawn: 8109 (1965)
None preserved

3100 Series of 1938

A similar scheme to that introduced with the 8100 series was applied in 1938 to the larger boilered 3150 class, but only five were dealt with before the outbreak of World War 2 in 1939 caused the cancellation of the programme. The old frames were used, with new front ends with curved drop-ends, and the new boilers were of 225lb psi pressure, which allied to smaller coupled wheels of 5ft 3in diameter gave a tractive effort of 31,170lb at 85 per cent — very desirable for the banking duties the engines were intended for.

The engines were rebuilt as follows:

No 3100 (frames ex 3173) Swindon 1938
No 3101 (frames ex 3156) Swindon 1939
No 3102 (frames ex 3181) Swindon 1939
No 3103 (frames ex 3155) Swindon 1939
No 3104 (frames ex 3179) Swindon 1939

In August 1939 Nos 3170 had been withdrawn for rebuilding as No 3105, but the scheme was abandoned and the engine returned to stock in original form.

First of class withdrawn: 3100 (1957)
Last of class withdrawn: 3103 (1960)
None preserved.

Bottom right: A scheme to rebuild the 3150 series as smaller-wheeled banking engines was also curtailed by the outbreak of war in 1939, when only five locomotives had been so dealt with. In similar fashion to the 8100 class, just described. the rebuilds utilised the old frames but had new front ends and new boilers. Boiler pressure was 225lb psi and the wheel diameter of the coupled wheels was 5ft 3in, in view of their intended duties. Later years saw them on passenger duties such as No 3100 is seen on here — a Porthcawl train at Cardiff General in August 1951. Note the upper lamp bracket located on the smokebox door, a feature of these engines. At this date the steps had not been welded to the bunker side./*P. Ransome-Wallis*

Below left: A plan to rebuild 40 5100 and 10 5101 class locomotives was curtailed when only 10 engines had been dealt with, due to the outbreak of war. The rebuilding utilised the frames of withdrawn 5100 engines, with new front ends and new boilers of higher pressure. The coupled wheel diameter was reduced to 5ft 6in to improve acceleration. No 8106 is seen in ex-works green livery with the small GWR monogram. The engine retains a tall safety valve bonnet, painted green, and has a whistle shield fitted./*C. R. L. Coles*

Below: Another photograph taken alongside the A shop at Swindon, showing No 8109 freshly overhauled as late as April 14, 1963, as a result of which it survived as last of the class for a further two years. The use of plain black livery at this late date is of note, although the chimney has a high polish on the copper cap. The class underwent very little visible alteration throughout its life span. No 8100 was in fact rebuilt from No 99 of 1903 (see page 43) which had subsequently been renumbered 3100 and 5100, thereby continuing Churchward's own policy of progressive development and improvement to the standard types. /*G. Wheeler*

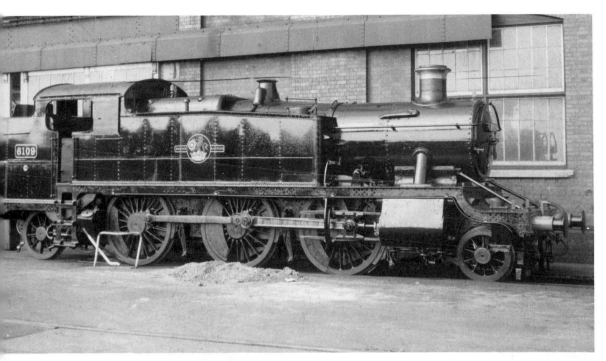

SECTION 4

4400 class 2-6-2T
Light Tank Engines

Introduced: 1904
Total: 11
GWR Classification: B (16½in cylinders) C
(17in cylinders) Uncoloured*
BR Power Class : 3MT

Intended primarily for branch-line work, where route restrictions prohibited the use of heavier locomotives, the prototype of these light 2-6-2Ts, No 115, appeared in 1905. It had a new coned standard No 5 boiler with a working pressure of 165lb psi and it could be described as a smaller edition of No 99 (see page 43), with 16½in by 24in outside cylinders and 4ft 1½in coupled wheels, and a pony truck at each end. The design was extremely successful, with the small wheels giving remarkable acceleration. The No 5 boiler had a total heating surface of 1272.6sq ft, consisting of a tube heating surface of 1176.9sq ft and a firebox heating surface of 95.7sq ft. The grate area was 16.83sq ft. With a tank capacity of 1000 gallons, the prototype weighed 55 tons 15cwt in full working order. Tractive effort was 18,515lb at 85 per cent. Ten production engines followed, and they were generally similar. They were constructed at Wolverhampton, which badly needed new work but was unable to handle the proposed larger engines (even the 2-6-2Ts proved difficult to handle); they were the first production version of one of Churchward's prototypes to be ordered.

With the addition of superheating, which took place over a prolonged period, from 1915 to 1927, the boiler pressure was increased to 180lb psi and the total heating surface was 1215.52sq ft, with the tubes giving 1019.69 sq ft, the firebox 94.12sq ft and the superheater 101.71sq ft. Tractive effort was increased to 20.195lb at 85 per cent with the 16½in-diameter cylinders and to 21.440lb with the later 17in cylinders.

*A yellow disc was painted on some engines, presumably in error.

These attractive little engines were long associated with the Cornish branch lines, and the Princetown branch was a favourite haunt. The bleak windswept line up to Dartmoor had numerous steep grades and sharp curves, and flange wear on the coupled wheels was a problem. Two experiments were made with oiling devices for reducing flange wear, on No 4402 in 1931 and No 4407 later, but neither proved successful, as the oil reached the wheel tyres and hence the rails, causing the locomotives to slip badly. Other areas they worked included the Porthcawl branch and the Much Wenlock branch.

The engines were built as follows:
No 115 (4400)   Swindon   1904
Nos 3101-3110
(4401-4410) Wolverhampton 1905-06

First of class withdrawn: 4402 (1949)
Last of class withdrawn: 4405/6/10 (1955)
None preserved.

Top right: Churchward's second prototype 2-6-2T No 115 was in effect a scaled-down version of his No 99 and proved equally successful. Built at Swindon in 1904 the engine had a half-coned standard taper boiler and slender cast-iron chimney. The small bunker had a straight back and toolboxes were mounted on the platform above the cylinders. Ten additional locomotives followed in 1905-6, built at Wolverhampton, and were numbered 3101-3110; they were generally similar, with short smokeboxes and cast-iron chimneys. No 115 became No 4400 and Nos 3101-3110 became Nos 4401-4410 respectively. An early modification was a small extension of the bunker to increase capacity./*British Rail*

Centre right: Further modifications took place over a lengthy period, and this photograph of No 4409 displays most obviously the extended smokebox, superheated boiler with top feed added, further extension to coal bunker, and copper-cap chimney (fitted about 1910-11). In fact the bunker extension dates from 1924, when the rear end was extended by about 9in, but at that time the locomotive had still not received front end struts. The copper-cap chimneys were replaced again by cast iron pattern, and a further modification to the bunker was provision of a recessed rear fender to accommodate the upper lamp bracket./ *Ian Allan Library*

Bottom right: Outside steam pipes were fitted to 5 of the 11 engines, in three cases with new curved drop-ends (Nos 4400/ 7/10), while two retained square drop ends (Nos 4406/8). Short safety valve bonnets and sliding cab shutters were later modifications and No 4408, pictured here in Tondu shed, also shows the front end struts. Photographed on September 9, 1951, by which time withdrawal of the class had started./ *H. C. Casserley*

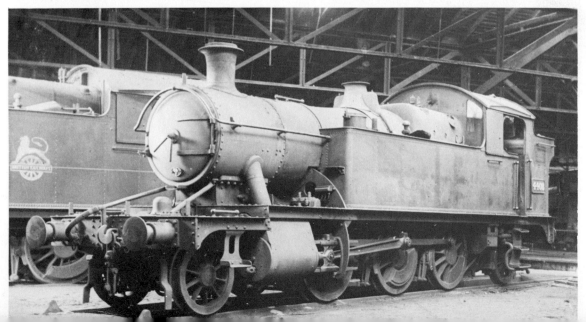

3800 Class: 2cyl 4-4-0
(County class)
Passenger Engines

Introduced : 1904
Total : 40
GWR Classification : C, Red

Despite the excellent work being performed by the Dean double-framed 4-4-0s, as modernised by Churchward, the standardisation scheme of 1901 envisaged an outside-cylinder standard 4-4-0 for future use. One route where such an engine would be useful was the Shrewsbury and Hereford line over which there were LNWR objections to the use of 4-6-0s at that time. In fact, the prototype, No 3473, was a shortened version of the prototype 4-6-0 No 98 and had the 6ft 8½in coupled wheels, 18in by 30in outside cylinders and many other parts in common. The boiler was a standard No 4, as also carried by the City class inside-cylinder 4-4-0s, which were produced at about the same time.

The usual period of prototype testing appears to have been curtailed somewhat, as a further 10 locomotives followed shortly, and were basically similar. As built, No 3473 had a total heating surface of 1818.12sq ft, consisting of a tube heating surface of 1689.82sq ft and a firebox heating surface of 128.30sq ft. The grate area was 20.56sq ft and the boiler pressure was 200lb psi. Tractive effort at 85 per cent was 20.530lb, and the weight of engine and tender in full working order was 92 tons 1cwt, with the 3000-gallon tender weighing 36 tons 15cwt.

Below: Second of the County class to be built, No 3474 *County of Berks*, with narrow cast-iron chimney and non-superheated boiler. The oval brass works plate is clearly visible below the smokebox, a feature discontinued at the end of 1911, when the plates on existing engines were also removed. The tender was of 3000 gallons capacity. On this initial batch of 10 engines, Nos 3473-82 (later renumbered 3800/3831-9), the sandboxes, for the driving wheels only, were located below the footplate. They were fitted with the steam brake and some of the brake rigging was outside the coupled wheels. The chimney is not the original fitted to the engine./*British Rail*

Top right: The first batch of engines were delivered with copper-cap chimneys of the small type seen here on No 3475 *County of Wilts*, but these were very soon replaced by the cast-iron variety. This driver's-side view clearly shows the arrangement of the reversing lever, the crosshead vacuum pump, and the brake rigging, and somehow emphasises the clean external finish, characteristic of Churchward's locomotives before superheating and top feed were introduced./*H. Gordon Tidey*

Centre right: The final batch of 10 County class 4-4-0s emerged in somewhat different form, with curved drop ends to the footplating, copper-cap chimneys, screw reverse and superheated boilers with top feed. The tender held 3500 gallons. This batch was numbered 3821-30 and came out in late 1911/early 1912. No 3826 *County of Flint* is illustrated here, with bogie brakes removed. The sandboxes of this batch (and the earlier Nos 3801-20) fed both driving and trailing coupled wheels, and projected above the footplating. This version of the County class had considerable similarity to the 4300 2-6-0s, showing H. Holcroft's influence upon the external appearance of the later Churchward engines./*Ian Allan Library*

Bottom right: Ten locomotives, Nos 3801-10, were named after Irish counties. One of the batch No 3809 *County Wexford*, was photographed at Old Oak Common in 1919, by which time the engine carried a superheated boiler and top feed, and larger diameter chimney. Superheating of the existing locomotives started in 1909 and about the same time the smokebox was extended forward by 9in. No 3809 shows the ATC apparatus below the bufferbeam, with conduit running along the valance to the cab. This had been applied to No 3809 as early as 1908 (and to Nos 3803/4/7) and all members of the class with the exception of Nos 3831/2, had received ATC by the end of their careers./*A. B. MacLeod*

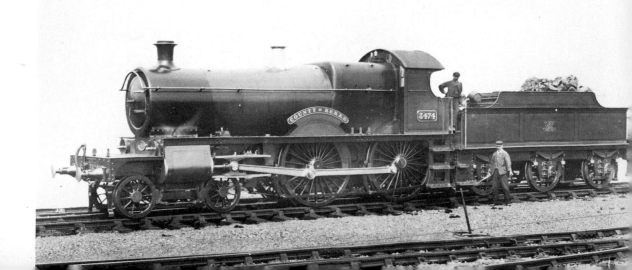

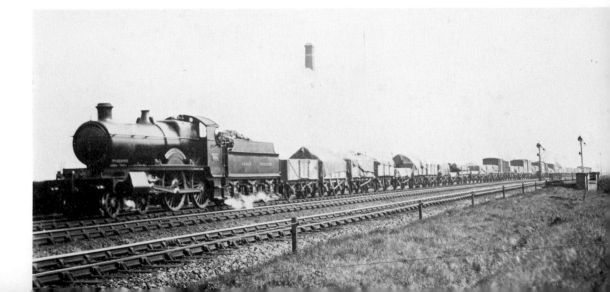

The combination of large outside cylinders and a short coupled wheelbase resulted in a tendency for the engines to roll quite badly, and they quickly gained a reputation for rough riding compared to the inside-cylinder City class, where the stroke of the cylinder was 26in, compared to 30in for the County class, and the ride was much smoother at speed. Despite the poor riding, Churchward persisted with the design and a further batch appeared, with 3500-gallon tenders weighing 40 tons full; they were Nos 3801-20 and had vacuum cylinders instead of the steam brake. Superheating and extended smokeboxes were applied to the class from 1909.

An interesting experimental rebuilding took place in November 1907, when No 3805 appeared with a standard No 2 boiler of the type carried by the Bulldog 4-4-0s, with a special plate frame bogie, in which state it ran for about two years.

In retrospect, this was probably the least successful of the Churchward standard classes, and seems to have been produced from a desire to standardise rather than from real need for such an engine. The building of a further batch of 10 in the winter of 1911-12 is all the more surprising, in view of the fact that by that time the new 4-6-0s were ousting the 4-4-0 classes from principal express duties. The final batch had detail differences, including screw reverse, superheated boilers with top feed, and a cylinder centre line coincident with the centre line of the coupled axles.

The engines were built as follows:

Nos 3473-3482	Swindon	1904
(3800/3831-3839)		
Nos 3801-3820	Swindon	1906
Nos 3821-3830	Swindon	1911-12

This was the first of the Churchward standard designs to be relegated to lesser duties, and their early withdrawal with the 4-4-2T tank engine version (see page 60), compared to his other classes is all the more poignant in that many of the Dean/Churchward 4-4-0s outlived them.

First of class withdrawn: 3833 (1930)
Last of class withdrawn: 3834 (1933)
None preserved.

Top left: County class No 3804 *County Dublin* makes a fine picture passing Sonning Box with a down Weymouth express on July 16, 1926. The circular spectacle plates are still in use over the firebox top, a feature of Churchward's engines which was abandoned by Collett. ATC gear is clearly visible below the bufferbeam./*M. W. Earley*

Centre left: In the austerity livery which originated in late 1914-18 war days, with all polished metal ornamentation painted over (except the brass beading, name and numberplates), but nevertheless spotlessly clean, No 3828 *County of Hereford* shows off the attractive lines of the final batch of engines. The engine retains the bogie brakes and has no ATC apparatus./*Ian Allan Library*

Bottom left: A freight train of about 50 wagons, hauled by No 3821 *County of Bedford*, passing Hayes. Such loads were a real test of the adhesion and brake power of four-coupled locomotives, and required skilful handling by the train crews. With a fixed wheelbase of only 8ft 6in and outside cylinders, oscillation was a marked feature of Churchward's County class, and they were known to the enginemen as habitual rough-riders./*H. Gordon Tidey*

Below: End of the line for Nos 3801 *County Carlow* and 3823 *County of Carnarvon*, photographed in partially dismantled condition on Swindon dump, May 17, 1931. The class had a relatively short life, with the first engine going in February 1930 and the last in November 1933, being ousted by the new breed of mixed-traffic 4-6-0 Hall class engines, introduced by Collett. Judging from this photograph certain parts of the engines were subsequently re-used by Swindon./*H. C. Casserley*

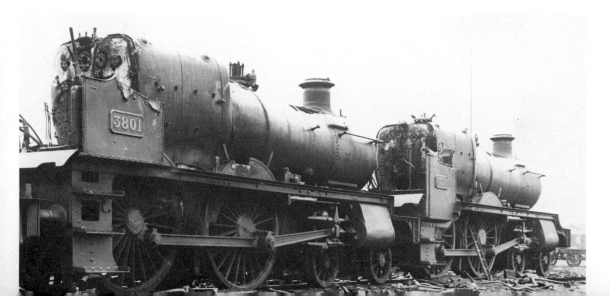

2221 class 4-4-2T
(County Tanks)
Passenger Tank Engines

Introduced : 1905
Total : 30
GWR Classification : C, Red

Basically a tank engine version of the County class 4-4-0s, it was inevitable that the 2221 class should be referred to, unofficially, as the County Tanks. In fact, the main difference was the boiler, which was the smaller standard No 2 design. The use of large 6ft $8\frac{1}{2}$in coupled wheels for a tank engine was an indication of the semi-fast outer-suburban duties they were intended for. No prototype was considered necessary and, as in the case of the County class, an initial batch of 10 appeared, in 1905-06.

The cylinders were of the usual 18in diameter by 30in stroke and the boiler pressure was 195lb psi. The total heating surface was 1517.89sq ft, with the tubes providing 1396.58sq ft and the firebox 121.31sq ft. The grate area was 20.35sq ft; total weight of the engine in working order, with 2000 gallons and 3 tons of coal, was 75 tons. A second batch, Nos 2231-40, was generally similar and appeared in 1908-09.

The last of the first batch, No 2230, was experimentally fitted with a standard No 4 boiler, which did not prove satisfactory, for weight

Below: No 2226 of the 1905-6 batch of 10 locomotives, with small plain cast-iron chimney and long-cone non-superheated boiler. The first locomotive built, No 2221, differed in having the cab sides flush with the side tanks and coal bunker, and had the numberplates on the tank sides; it was also fitted for a while with steam sanding gear. No 2225 of this batch ran for a while, from July 1909, in an experimental crimson lake livery. The locomotive illustrated here shows the square drop ends to the framing, a feature of Nos 2221 – 40 inclusive, and the semi-circular ducting on the tank tops, which formed part of the two-way water pick-up apparatus with which the whole class was fitted until late 1921./*Ian Allan Library*

Right: The second batch of engines appeared in 1908-9 and were numbered 2231-40. They were basically the same as the preceding 10 when new, and engines of both batches received superheated boilers during 1910-14; top feed was also added. No 2237 is illustrated in latter-day condition, with extended bunker, cast-iron chimney (when new Nos 2231-40 had copper-cap chimneys) and circular spectacle plates removed from above firebox. No 2230 of the earlier batch ran for a short period with the larger No 4 standard boiler, as an experiment, but there were no major alterations to the 20 locomotives of the first two batches, which remained different in some respects to the final 10 engines, throughout their relatively short careers. The two-way water pick-up apparatus had been removed from No 2237 by the time this superb photograph was taken./*M. W. Earley*

Below right: The third and final batch of locomotives, Nos 2241-50, appeared in 1912 and differed from the earlier construction in having curved drop ends to the front footplating, superheated boilers with top feed, and an extended smokebox with large diameter chimney with copper cap. No 2247 is seen here with the original bunker and with the two circular spectacle plates above the firebox. Bunkers were enlarged by extending the top backwards in the period 1922-5, and the spectacle plates were blanked off. The centre lines of the coupled wheels and cylinders were coincident on this final batch; previous engines had them offset. The engine still had two-way water pick-up apparatus fitted when this picture was taken./*Ian Allan Library*

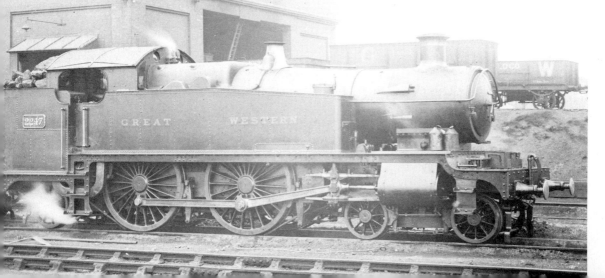

reasons, and was quickly removed. Super-heating of the 2221-2240 series was under-taken between 1910-14 and top feed was added. The last batch of engines appeared in 1912, and as in the case of the County 4-4-0s they had the Holcroft-style curved drop ends at the front and were built new with super-heaters, top feed and extended smokeboxes. The centre lines of the cylinders and coupled-wheel axles were coincident. With superheating, the total combined heating surface was 1316.14sq ft, with the tubes pro-viding 1009.26sq ft, the firebox 122.13sq ft and the superheater 184.75sq ft. The boiler pressure for the entire class was standardised at 200lb, at the end of 1919, and this gave a tractive effort of 20,530lb.

The class was mainly associated with London area services, although they were tried out elsewhere, and the arrival of the Collett 6100 version of Churchward's 2-6-2T design, in the early 1930s, displaced them. They seem to have been early candidates for withdrawal for the same basic reason as their tender counterpart, namely, that they were not as versatile as the six-coupled engines of the Churchward standard range.

The engines were built as follows:

Nos 2221-2230	Swindon	1905-06
Nos 2231-2240	Swindon	1908-09
Nos 2241-2250	Swindon	1912

Above: A slender cast-iron chimney had replaced the original version when No 2244 was photographed at Slough on May 17, 1930. The small air vent on the tank top alongside the firebox was introduced when the two-way water pick-up apparatus was removed (about 1921) and the bunker had been enlarged. No 2244 was withdrawn just three years and three months later, by which time the class was being rapidly replaced by the superior new 6100 2-6-2Ts (see page 49) which had been specially developed by Collett for the accelerated London suburban trains, introduced by the GWR to combat increasing road competition./ *H. C. Casserley*

Above right: Although none of the class ever carried names, they were usually referred to as County Tanks. They spent most of their existence on London area workings, and No 2249 makes a typical picture standing at Paddington, bunker-first. One locomotive, No 2243, which was withdrawn from service in December 1934 – by which time only a handful survived – in fact remained intact for a further five years, being retained as a stationary boiler for carriage heating at Old Oak Common; it was not despatched to the Swindon dump until mid-1939./ *P. Ransome-Wallis*

Right: As already mentioned, the rear of the bunker was enlarged from 1922-5, and in addition a plain back fender was added (in one or two cases it had appeared on the original bunker design). No 2222 displays this feature, at Aylesbury on March 15, 1930. Some engines had the fender recessed in later years, to hold the upper lamp bracket, and in one or two cases the recess was carried down the bunker extensions./ *H. C. Casserley*

First of class withdrawn: 2228 (1931)
Last of class withdrawn: 2246 (1935)*
None preserved.

*No 2243 survived as a stationary boiler until 1939.

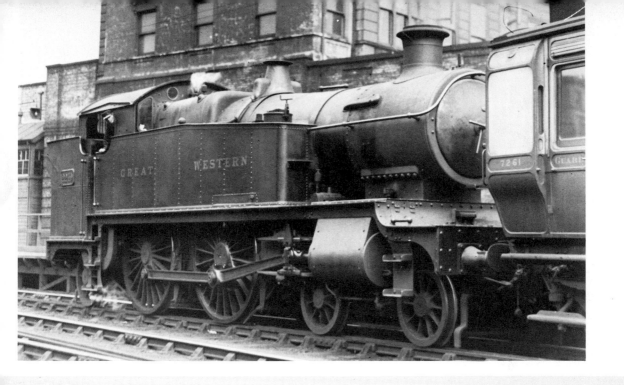

SECTION 7

4000 class ; 4-cyl 4-6-0 (The Stars)
Express Passenger Engines

Introduced: 1906
Total: 73
GWR Classification: D, Red
BR Power Class: 5P

Churchward's masterpiece, the Star class, was the product of intelligent analysis of existing practices and foresight of future requirements. He proceeded cautiously at first, with his two-cylinder engines competing against the imported French compound *La France*. The provision of a divided drive between two axles on the four-cylinder French 4-4-2 appealed to him, but the complexities of the compound system did not. He decided to put in hand the design of a four-cylinder simple express passenger engine, with boiler pressure and wheel arrangement similar to the De Glehn-Du Bousquet imports, of which the two later and larger engines Nos 103/4 were in service. Consequently the prototype, No 40, was a 4-4-2 of a completely new type, with a novel scissors-type valve gear to operate the four cylinders, of which the chief feature was that the oscillation of each expansion link was derived from the reciprocation of the main crosshead on the opposite side of the engine.

Below: The drawing shows a Star in later condition, with top feed, but without outside steampipes to the cylinders.

Top right: By 1906 Churchward had gained sufficient experience with his two-cylinder 4-4-2s and 4-6-0s running alongside the French Compounds to enable him to proceed with a further development, which acknowledged that compounding was not of significant value in GWR conditions. The Swindon locomotives, with high-pressure boilers and long valve travel, had proved to be as economical as the French 4-4-2s. The latter, however, were seen to be the smoother running engines, due to the four-cylinder layout and the divided drive over two axles. The next development was therefore a four-cylinder simple 4-4-2 which amalgamated the best of Swindon and French practice. No 40 *North Star* (the name was added five months after completion) emerged from Swindon in May 1906, and carried the first long-cone standard No 1 boiler, with 225lb psi working pressure. No 40 had a number of features which remained unique while it ran as a 4-4-2 compared to its successors in the Star class, including the unusual scissors valve gear, and fluted coupling rods. Seen here in new condition, prior to naming, with small-diameter copper-capped chimney and swing-link bogie. Note the maker's plate on leading splasher, and the location of the sandbox./*Ian Allan Library*

Centre right: A later picture of No 40, still running as a 4-4-2. The original chimney has been replaced by one of larger diameter with capuchon and beading has been added to the splashers. The nameplate has the Swindon works plate below it, on the trailing splasher. The square drop ends to the framing and the box-like housing for the inside cylinders are emphasised in this view. No 40 ran as an Atlantic for just over three years. Meanwhile, Churchward had opted for the 4-6-0 wheel arrangement for future express passenger locomotive development and the decision to proceed with further four-cylinder simple locomotives for fast express duties resulted in the production of the first batch of the famous Star class 4-6-0s./*Ian Allan Library*

Bottom right: No 4002 *Evening Star*, second of the initial batch of 10 locomotives, illustrated in shop grey livery. As first delivered, with slender chimney and safety valve bonnet, long-cone boiler devoid of external fittings and curved drop ends to the framing, these were exceptionally attractive modern-looking locomotives. The tender was of 3500 gallons capacity and matched the lines of the locomotive extremely well./*British Rail*

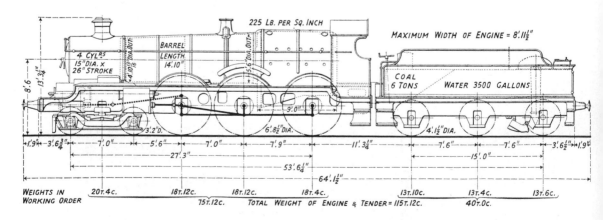

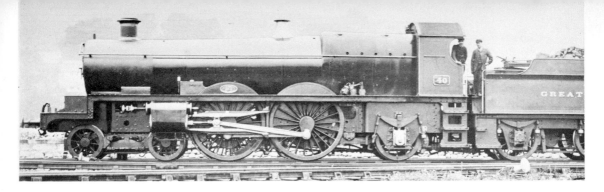

Top left: In this historic picture, taken at Euston during the exchange trials of 1910 (see page 10), No 4005 *Polar Star* has the later large diameter chimney, and the French-type bogie, introduced that year with Nos 4011-20 and gradually fitted to the earlier engines. The slidebars have a tie-rod between them. The paved track of the period is noteworthy, and what an immaculate spectacle the engine presented! The tender has the long side fenders fitted; it was in fact the first example of this modification./*British Rail*

Bottom left: From No 4001 onward, inside Walschaerts valve gear was adopted for all four cylinder engines, together with screw-operated reverse. No 4010 was delivered with a Cole superheater in 1909. No 4009 *Shooting Star* is illustrated with the Churchward version of the French De Glehn bogie which greatly improved the ride and has a 3500-gallon tender, with short side fenders./*Ian Allan Library*

Centre left: In 1908 a second batch of 10 engines was delivered, numbered 4011-20 and named after Knights. They had the improved bogies, and for a short while Nos 4011-6/8 carried front footsteps ahead of the cylinders (similar to those on *The Great Bear* when new, see page 78); Nos 4002/8/9 also were fitted during the same period: The footsteps were removed presumably because they limited the loading gauge availability to some degree. No 4011 was built new with a Swindon No 1 superheater (Field-tube type) which was replaced by the new standard type in 1910. No 4018 *Knight of the Grand Cross* is depicted here in original condition but with front footsteps removed./*Ian Allan Library*

Above: The names of English Kings were chosen for the batch of 10 locomotives delivered in 1909, Nos 4021-30. When new, No 4021 carried the first Swindon No 3 superheater, which was thenceforth adopted as standard. The following nine had non-superheated boilers and No 4030 was the last Star to be built new without a superheater; it was also the last to be built with the Swindon works plate on the splasher. No 4022 *King William* is seen in original condition, with saturated taper boiler and T-section slide bars with a tie-rod between them. The box-like casing over the two inside cylinders was altered on this batch of engines to a more graceful shape. *Ian Allan Library*

As built, No 40 had four cylinders of $14\frac{1}{4}$in diameter by 26in stroke and coupled wheels of 6ft $8\frac{1}{2}$in. The boiler was the first long coned example of the Swindon standard No 1 and had a total heating surface of 2142.91sq ft, consisting of a tube heating surface of 1988.65sq ft and a firebox heating surface of 154.26sq ft. The grate area was 27.07sq ft. Tractive effort was 25.090lb at 85 per cent and the engine and tender weighed 114 tons 10cwt in full working order, with the 3500-gallon tender weighing 40 tons.

This superb engine was so successful on trial that Churchward was able to proceed with confidence with an order for 10 more which appeared in 1907. He had meanwhile decided in favour of the 4-6-0 wheel arrangement, and produced a specially designed arrangement of the Walschaerts valve gear — to avoid the complications of the Scissors gear. In the new arrangement, set between the frames, two sets of gear were operated by two large eccentrics mounted on the leading coupled axle, between the two cranks. This design of valve gear remained standard for all four-cylinder GWR locomotives from then on, with the valves of the two outside cylinders operated by means of two horizontal cranked levers. Screw reverse was fitted.

This first batch of 10 4-6-0s were similar in respect of boiler dimensions and tractive effort, and weighed 115 tons 12cwt. They carried the names of the original broad-gauge Star class of 1839-41 and henceforth the new design was known as the Star class, No 40 receiving the name *North Star* (before conversion to a 4-6-0 in November 1909). A second batch of 10 followed in 1908 and had the improved bogie that Churchward developed from the De Glehn design on the

Top left: After the Kings came the Queens. The batch of 10 delivered late 1910/11 were Nos 4031-40 and carried the names of English Queens. They all had the standard superheater, of low-temperature type. No 4037 *Queen Philippa* had received top feed by the time this picture was taken. The 3500-gallon tenders were built new with the longer side fenders. In 1913 five more engines appeared, named after Princes and carried Nos 4041-5. The first of these had 15in cylinders which raised the tractive effort to 27,800lb. The boilers were delivered new with top feed, which by that time had also been fitted to all the existing standard No 1 boilers. Experience with the 15in cylinders on No 4041 *Prince of Wales* resulted in adoption of this feature for the rest of the class./*Ian Allan Library*

Centre left: No 4056 *Princess Margaret*, built in May 1914, is seen here in late World War 1 condition (about 1917/8) with plain green livery devoid of lining and with chimney cap and safety valve casing painted over. The ornamental brass rims of the driving wheel splashers have been removed. This batch of Stars Nos 4046-60 (all delivered in May 1914) had I-section coupling rods when new (as seen here) but they were later replaced by rectangular-section rods. They also had the larger 15in cylinders. The more graceful housing for the inside cylinders had first appeared on Nos 4021-30. This batch of engines was the first to receive the four-cone ejector, adopted as standard equipment for large passenger engines./*Ian Allan Library*

Bottom left: The final batch of Stars, Nos 4061-72, were built at Swindon in 1922/3 and the names was those of Abbeys on the Great Western system. Churchward had retired at the end of 1921, and Collett might well have made some of the detail alterations to this final dozen engines. They were delivered with plain cast-iron chimneys and carried the economy plain green livery devoid of lining or brass trim to the splashers. The bogie brakes seen here on No 4063 *Bath Abbey* were removed, during the general removal of bogie brakes in 1923-5, after tests by Collett showed them to have little value./*Ian Allan Library*

Above: After three years in service as a 4-4-2 No 40 *North Star* was converted to a 4-6-0 in November 1909. The engine received new frames, with the curved drop ends and more graceful cylinder cover at the front, and the boiler was one of the older short-cone variety updated with superheater. Renumbered 4000 in December 1912, the engine is seen here with the additions of top feed and four-cone ejector and French-type bogie. This was one of the engines selected by Collett for rebuilding as Castle class (see Appendix 1). The engine remained unique in having the platform 2½in higher than the rest of the class, thereby completely clearing the top of the outside cylinders./*Ian Allan Library*

French engines. They were followed by further batches, No 4041 appearing with 15in cylinders instead of 14¼in.

Some doubts were expressed about the ability of the boiler to steam four 15in cylinders, but Churchward proved otherwise and the entire class was eventually fitted with them. After some initial experiments on Nos 4010/1 superheaters became standard equipment from 1913 onwards. The tube heating surface then became 1599.4sq ft, the firebox 155.0sq ft and the superheater 260.0sq ft, making a total of 2014.4sq ft. With the 15in cylinders the tractive effort was raised to 27,800lb at 85 per cent.

The Stars were extremely free running engines and continued to work express passenger turns for their entire career. The basic design was enlarged by Collett to produce the Castle and later the King class four-cylinder 4-6-0s, and it would be fair to claim that for an engine produced in 1907 they were at least 20 years ahead of their time.

As the illustrations show, there were many detail changes over the years, with two different styles of outside steam pipes, and tenders of 3000, 3500 and 4000 gallons capacity. Between 1925 and 1940, 16 of the class were reconstructed as Castles and they are dealt with in Appendix 1. When new, the Stars were fitted with equalisers between the springs of the six coupled wheels, but they were replaced by the use of more flexible springs in later years. *North Star* retained the scissors-type valve gear until withdrawn for conversion to a Castle class engine in 1929.

The engines were built as follows:

No 40 (4000)	Swindon	1906
Nos 4001-4010	Swindon	1907
Nos 4011-4020	Swindon	1908
Nos 4021-4030	Swindon	1909

Nos 4031-4040	Swindon	1910-11
Nos 4041-4045	Swindon	1913
Nos 4046-4060	Swindon	1914
Nos 4061-4072	Swindon	1922-23

First of class withdrawn[*]: 4006, 4011 (1932)
Last of class withdrawn : 4056 (1957)
Example preserved : 4003

[*]Excluding locomotives withdrawn for conversion to Castle class, see Appendix 1.

Above: Fresh from overhaul at Swindon in October 1951, and carrying fully lined BR green livery, No 4049 *Princess Maud* has the Castle-type outside steam pipes to the cylinders. The engine is coupled to a 4000-gallon tender. Other tender variations over the years included 4045/22 coupled to the bogie tender off *The Great Bear* (in 1936) and 4043 with the unique eight-wheel Collett tender. In post-WW II days Nos 4058/62 were attached to Hawksworth flat-sided tenders for a while. The top lamp bracket has been transferred to the smokebox door and engine has a large-diameter chimney and squat safety valve bonnet./*R. H. G. Simpson*

Above right: No 4056 *Princess Margaret* is seen here in late condition, running in BR lined green passenger livery, in May 1952. Changes over the years have included provision of elbow-type outside steam pipes; safety valve casing of reduced height; rectangular-section coupling rods; removal of bogie brakes; provision of whistle shield; removal of small porthole cab windows over firebox; and provision of 4000-gallon tender. The engine was photographed on a down train near Wootton Bassett; it survived to be last of the class when withdrawn in October 1957./*J. F. Russell-Smith*

Right: Comparison with the foregoing picture of *Princess Maud* shows No 4062 *Malmesbury Abbey* (also seen at Swindon, on June 15, 1952) to have various detail differences. In particular the outside steam pipes are of elbow type, curving back between the frames, and there is a Collett-style housing to the screw reverse ahead of the cab. The rear coupled wheels have a speedometer fitted, a feature applied from 1937 onward. The tender is of 4000 gallons capacity./*R. C. Riley*

4500, 4575 class 2-6-2T
Light Tank Engines

Introduced: 1906
Total: 175
GWR Classification: C, Yellow
BR Power Class: 4MT

Experience with the 4400 class in service (see page 54) suggested that an increase in coupled wheel diameter would make them more generally useful engines, by giving them an added turn of speed. The general dimensions remained unaltered, and 20 locomotives were delivered from Wolverhampton during 1906-08, with 4ft 7½in coupled wheels and 17in diameter by 24in stroke cylinders. The boiler pressure was 180lb psi and tractive effort was 19,120lb at 85 per cent. The weight in full working order was 57 tons, with a tank capacity of 1000 gallons. They were the last new locomotives to be constructed at Wolverhampton, as the decision was taken to concentrate building at Swindon.

The second batch of 10, Nos 2181-90, were therefore Swindon-built, and had the boiler pressure increased to 200lb, with a tractive effort of 21,250lb. Superheaters were fitted to existing locomotives from 1913, and

Below: The drawing depicts the 4575 series.

Top right: A beautiful photograph, once issued as a commercial local view postcard, depicting 2-6-2T No 2179 at Lustleigh Station. This engine was one of the original batch of Wolverhampton-built locomotives Nos 2161-2180 (later Nos 4500-4519) of 1906-8, and in fact was the last but one locomotive ever constructed by Wolverhampton Works after the decision was taken to concentrate all new work at Swindon. The early engines of the class had their numberplates on the tank sides, as shown here, and this particular example has received a superheated boiler, top feed and small extension to the bunker. The chimney is copper capped and the tall brass safety valve bonnet positively sparkles. One could scarcely wish for a more idyllic scene./*Ian Allan Library*

Centre right: No 4516, originally No 2177, showing the numberplate transferred to the bunker, which is of the slightly enlarged type. The original location of the numberplate is still fairly easily discernable between the lettering on the tank side. The engine has had front end struts added and has top feed with tall safety valve bonnet. One locomotive of this batch, No 4515, had a unique sloping coal bunker, somewhat similar to that used on the 1361 class (see page 104), a feature it carried until 1927./*Ian Allan Library*

Bottom right: Starting about 1924 the bunker was extended 9in by means of distance pieces between the original rear buffer beam and a new one. It increased bunker capacity to 3 tons 14cwt, and can be seen on this picture of No 4509, which then still carried a toolbox above the cylinders./*Ian Allan Library*

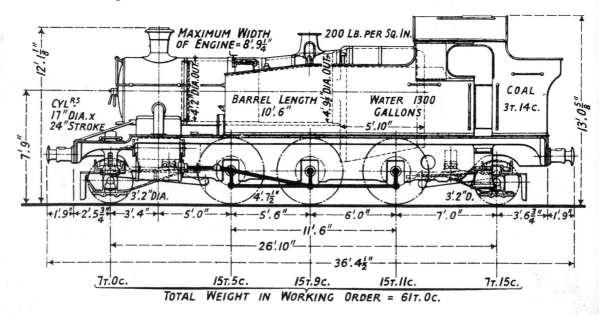

Below: A classic picture of No 4564, at work on a St Ives train at Carbis Bay. The locomotive is in BR lined green livery, but otherwise surprisingly little altered over the years. From No 4534 onwards the engines had curved drop ends, and from 4555-74 (of 1924) outside steampipes, cast-iron chimneys and enlarged bunkers when new. Outside steam pipes were fitted to many of the earlier engines over the years, in some cases retaining the square drop ends of the original Churchward design./*John Ashman*

Right: Another view of No 4564, this time with a goods train bound for Gloucester on the Cinderford Branch on August 28, 1964. This delightful picture clearly shows the recessed fender at the rear of the coal bunker./*B. J. Ashworth*

Bottom: Raking sunlight on the front end of No 4507, photographed at Swindon shed on December 20, 1959. The engine had outside steampipes, but retained the square drop ends./*Dr. J. A. Coiley*

were fitted new to Nos 4540-4554 of 1914-15. This gave a total combined heating surface of 1215.52sq ft, with a tube heating surface of 1019.69 sq ft, a firebox heating surface of 94.12 sq ft and a superheater heating surface of 101.71sq ft. Minor alterations took place on subsequent engines, and Nos 4555-4574 were built new with outside steam pipes, enlarged bunkers and improved superheaters.

A final batch of 100 engines was delivered between 1927-29, with increased water capacity of 1300 gallons housed in larger tanks, with a sloping top to the front end. The weight was thereby increased to 61 tons, and the series was referred to as the 4575 class.

Essentially designed for branch line working, these delightful little engines were an everyday feature of the West Country scene. When new, Nos 2165-2167 were renumbered 31-33 then transferred to the Rhondda and Swansea Bay Railway, where they remained for some time. Nos 2165/6 were similarly transferred to the Port Talbot Railway. The 4575 series, with increased water capacity, were more widespread in their activities, working a variety of local and branch services around Bristol, Worcester, Neath and Wolverhampton, while a few were employed on Paddington empty stock duties for a number of years, before being replaced by pannier tanks.

The engines were built as follows:

Nos 2161-2180		
(4500-4519)	Wolverhampton	1906-08
Nos 2181-2190		
(4520-4529)	Swindon	1909-10
Nos 4530-4539	Swindon	1913
Nos 4540-4554	Swindon	1914-15
Nos 4555-4574	Swindon	1924

Nos 4575-4599 } 5500-5504 }	Swindon	1927
Nos 5505-5524	Swindon	1927
Nos 5525-5544	Swindon	1928
Nos 5545-5574	Swindon	1928-29

First of class withdrawn: 4531 (1950)
Last of class withdrawn: 5508, 5531, 5564, 5569 (1964)
Examples preserved: 4555, 4561, 4566, 4588.

Below: In the period 1927-29 a further 100 locomotives were constructed, with larger side tanks holding 1300 gallons; the tanks had sloping tops at the forward end, adding to the rakish appearance of the engines. Known as the 4575 class they were numbered 4575-5574 and were somewhat heavier than the earlier 4500 locomotives. No 5503 is seen here, with tall safety valve bonnet; from No 5545 onwards the engines were built new with the smaller bonnet, a feature which slowly spread to other locomotives of the class. The sliding cab shutters had yet to be fitted when this picture was taken./ *Ian Allan Library*

Top right: During 1953 auto apparatus was fitted to 15 of the 4575 series, for push-pull services in the Cardiff Valleys and Bridgend area. These were Nos 4578/80/1/9, 5511/24/7/9/34/45/55/60/8/72/4. Seen here is No 4589 at Cardiff Queen St on October 6, 1953, working the 2.10pm train from Coryton to Cardiff Bute Rd. with the locomotive propelling the train./ *S. Rickard*

Centre right: Auto-fitted 4575 2-6-2T No 5545 at Shrewsbury on September 24, 1960. It was one of the last survivors of the class and carried fully lined BR green livery. The rear-of-bunker recessed housing for the upper lamp bracket can be seen, also auto apparatus below the footplate. This and the following photograph of No 5551 show the final condition of this notable series of light 2-6-2Ts./*J. C. Haydon*

Bottom right: These attractive and sprightly little tank engines received fully lined-out BR green livery in their last years of service, and very well it suited them! No 5551 was fresh from the Swindon painter's hands when photographed on April 12, 1959, and certainly looked younger than its 31 years of service. Such was the rapid demise of steam at that time, however, that No 5551 was destined to last only 11 more months in service before withdrawal./*G. Wheeler*

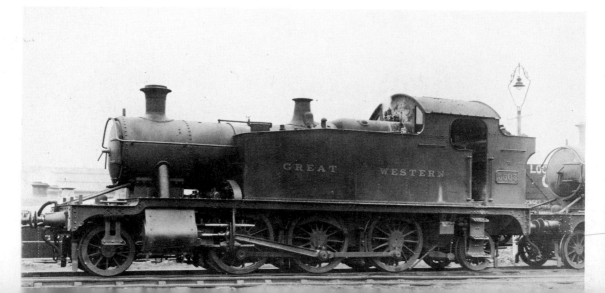

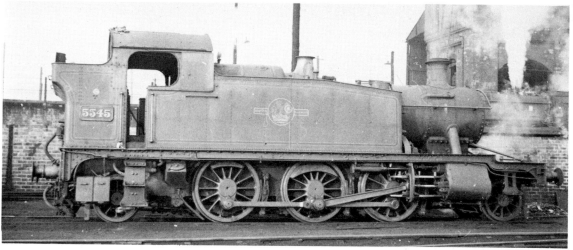

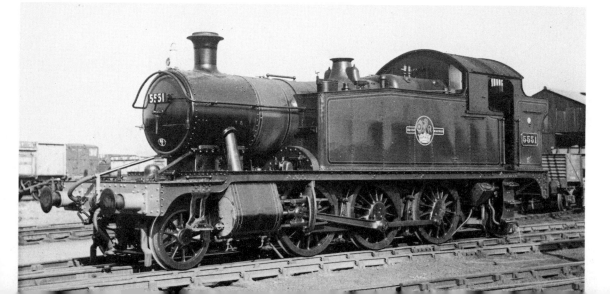

No III, 4-cyl 4-6-2
The Great Bear
Express Passenger Engine

Introduced: 1908
Total: 1
GWR Classification: Special red, indicated by a black + on the red disc.

Few locomotives have been surrounded by such an air of mystery and intrigue as that which seems to accompany any attempt to explain why Churchward produced *The Great Bear*. The simple fact remains that Churchward was instructed to build the *largest* engine in the country by the GWR directors, who were seeking the advertising prestige this would undoubtedly produce. Churchward made it clear that it would be a costly engine and an engine very restricted in its use. He was nevertheless instructed to proceed with design and construction, as cheaply as possible. To do this he took his excellent Star class 4-6-0 as the basis, using standard cylinder castings, motion, bogie and coupled wheels. New frames and boiler were of course required and a trailing radial axle was added.

When No III *The Great Bear* appeared in January 1908 it was not only Britain's first 4-6-2 but also the third example of the type in Europe, and furthermore she was destined to remain the only British Pacific for 14 years. When unveiled to the GWR directors, at Paddington and to the public at large, the engine was received with considerable acclaim and certainly achieved the advertising aims of the exercise. In traffic, however, the story was different, with many teething troubles and very restricted route availability. Because of its sheer size and weight *The Great Bear* was only acceptable on the Paddington-Bristol main line, although recorded as having made solitary forays to Newton Abbot and Wolverhampton. Speed was limited to 65mph, which prevented any exhibition of real potential in that direction.

Below: In this official photograph of No 111 *The Great Bear* taken in February 1908 the locomotive carried footsteps ahead of the outside cylinders, but the steps tended to scrape platform edges when the engine was sent from Swindon to Paddington for the official inspection by GWR directors, so they were removed. The engine had a brass cap to the chimney, when new, and the boiler had a Swindon No 1 Field-tube 3-row superheater. No top feed was fitted, and the general external appearance was one of massive neatness, but the firebox end of the locomotive and narrow cab somehow seemed visually inadequate in proportion to the front end and boiler./*Ian Allan Library*

Right: With forward footsteps removed, but otherwise in original condition, No 111 *The Great Bear* makes a splendid picture as the locomotive heads a down Bristol express past Acton. The bogie tender was unique in GWR practice and certainly blended well with the massive proportions of the engine. By the time this photograph was taken, the cab roof had been shortened to allow the footplatemen more room to manipulate the fireirons./*H. Gordon Tidey*

Bottom right: In December 1913 the Pacific emerged from Swindon after a lengthy shopping during which top feed was added and the superheater replaced by a standard two-row pattern. By 1920 a 4-cone ejector was added and the brass — capped chimney with unlined green livery was replaced by a cast-iron version. Various attempts were made to alter and improve the weight distribution of the engine, which was not to the liking of the engineering department. The photograph shows No 111 in its last years, with unlined green livery and most metalwork painted over. The tender survived the engine and later ran coupled to various engines of the County, Saint and Star classes./*Ian Allan Library*

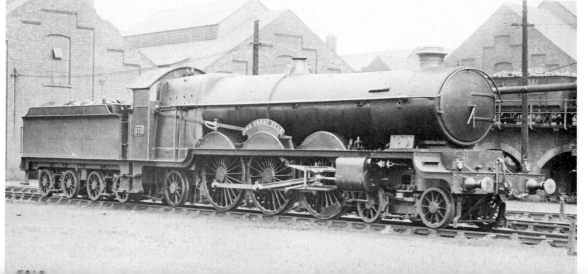

The engine had four cylinders 15in diameter by 26in stroke, with piston valves of 8in diameter and a maximum travel of $7\frac{1}{4}$in. The wheel diameters were coupled wheels 6ft $8\frac{1}{2}$in, bogie wheels 3ft 2in and trailing wheels 3ft 8in. The massive, but simple, boiler (known as standard No 6) had a total heating surface of 3400.81sq ft, consisting of a tube heating surface of 2673.45sq ft, arch tube heating surface of 24.22sq ft, firebox heating surface of 158.14sq ft and superheater of 545.sq ft. The grate area was 41.79sq ft and the boiler pressure was 225lb. Total weight of the engine and tender in full working order was 142 tons 15cwt, of which 45 tons 15cwt was applicable to the eight-wheeled bogie tender, which had a water capacity of 3500 gallons. Tractive effort was 27,800lb at 85 per cent. The bogie wheels on the engine and the tender wheels were of the same diameter, and the tender bogies were the same as the standard engine bogie except for a shortened wheelbase and absence of side bearers.

The Great Bear was always allocated to Old Oak Common shed, London, and worked Paddington-Bristol turns, including vacuum-fitted goods trains. The ability of the engine to handle the fitted goods led to the design of the 4700 class (see page 96). The weakest feature of the Pacific was the inside radial axleboxes at the trailing end, which were near the ashpan and tended to run hot. With that and the weight problems, which dictated a route availability so limited that it even included being barred from using No 1 platform at Paddington (having jumped the rails while backing on to trains there!), Collett decided to withdraw the engine at a time when expensive repairs were required to the boiler and firebox. In January 1924 it was dismantled for conversion to a Castle class 4-6-0 (see Appendix 1) and one of Britain's most historic engines ceased to exist.

No III was built at Swindon in 1908 and withdrawn for conversion in 1924.

A 14-coach load seems well suited to No 111's dimensions, and it is worth recalling that *The Great Bear* was visually a giant among British steam locomotives for many years after its construction. The engine is pictured in final condition, with top feed and cast-iron chimney, working the 10.45am express ex-Paddington, passing Twyford. It was a Gloucester and Cheltenham train which No 111 worked as far as Swindon. The total length of engine and tender over buffers was 71ft $2\frac{1}{4}$in compared to the 64ft $1\frac{1}{2}$in of a Star class 4-6-0./ *H. Gordon Tidey*

4200, 5205 class 2-8-0T
Mineral Tank Engines

Introduced: 1910
Total: 205†
GWR classification: E, Red.
BR Power Class: 7F*8F

In the early 1900s the developing mineral traffic in South Wales, with its characteristic of a short haul from pithead to port or power station, brought about the need for a tank engine version of the 2800 class tender locomotive. At first, a 2-8-2T design was contemplated, but the wheelbase was considered undesirably long and the design was finalised as a 2-8-0T. The usual practice of producing a prototype resulted in the appearance of No 4201 in 1910. As built it had two cylinders of 18½in diameter by 30in stroke and the superheated boiler had a heating surface of 1566.74sq ft, with the tubes providing 1228.02sq ft, the firebox 122.92sq ft and the superheater 215.80sq ft. No top feed was fitted. The leading pony wheels were 3ft 2in in diameter and the four coupled wheels were 4ft 7½in in diameter. The weight in full working order was 81 tons 12cwt, and tractive effort at 85 per cent was 31,450lb. The boiler pressure was 200lb psi. A small bunker was fitted with

* Nos 4200-5204 were 7F; Nos 5205-64 were 8F.
† The total includes locomotives delivered as 2-8-0T but rebuilt as 2-8-2T.

a capacity of only three tons and the water capacity was 1800 gallons.

The production version appeared with enlarged bunker capacity holding approximately half-a-ton more coal, and the boiler had top feed. The bunker on No 4201 was subsequently enlarged, about 1919, when a

Below: The drawing depicts the 5205 series. In this condition, with outside steam pipes and cylinders of 19in diameter by 30in stroke, the engines had a combined heating surface of 1670.15sq ft and a tractive effort of 33,170lb. This resulted in the BR power classification of 8F, compared to the 7F of Nos 4200-5204.

Top right: The pioneer 4200 class 2-8-0T, No 4201, was delivered in 1910, 14 months before production orders started and it differed in having a small straight-backed bunker and a copper-capped chimney, and no top feed. Such a small bunker for such a large locomotive clearly revealed the intended nature of the engine's duties, namely short-haul freight working./*Ian Allan Library*

Centre right: The production batches, Nos 4202-61 produced between 1912 and 1917, had top feed, enlarged coal bunkers and bi-directional rain strip on cab roof. The enlarged bunker held an extra half-ton or thereabouts of coal; a further modification to increase capacity was made from 1919 onwards, raising capacity to 4 tons 2cwt by lengthening the back end about six inches with inserted distance pieces. The following batches 4264-85 of 1919-20 and 4286-99, 5200-4 and 4200 of 1921-23 were generally similar with the enlarged bunker capacity, but had cast-iron chimneys, a feature applied to the earlier locomotives as time went on./*Ian Allan Library*

Bottom right: Outside steam pipes were introduced to the class with Nos 5205-14 built in 1923, and they also had cylinders of increased (19in) diameter. The next batch, Nos 5215-24, was generally similar, but had the frames lengthened at the rear from new. No 5223 is pictured in June 1951, with sliding shutters to cabside, short safety valve bonnet and lamp bracket on top of smokebox. The additional handrail on the stay over the boiler (connecting the two side tanks) is clearly visible and the smokebox door numberplate is missing, although the fixing brackets are there./*P. C. Short*

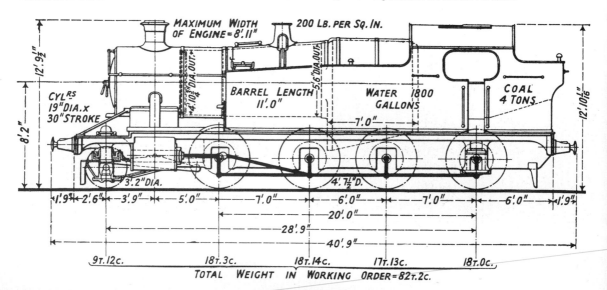

further general increase in bunker capacity, to 4 tons 2cwt, took place.

The depression of the late 1920s — early 1930s brought about a decline in the mineral traffic for which the class was built. Their small coal capacity rendered them unsuitable for long-distance work, and as a result selected examples had the frames extended at the rear to accommodate a radial axle and to carry a larger bunker containing an additional two tons of coal and 700 gallons of water. Thus the original 2-8-2T design of 1905

Top left: No 4257, ex-works at Swindon on February 7, 1960, showing the distance pieces inserted between the rear bufferbeam and running plate to enlarge bunker capacity, also the recessed rear of the bunker top, to carry the lamp bracket. The engine has received sliding cab shutters, and has a short safety valve bonnet and outside steam pipes./*Alec Swain*

Centre left: Nos 5275-94 of 1930 were delivered with a revised front end design, which had the platforms raised clear of the cylinders. These engines were stored from new, due to a decline in coal traffic, and between 1934 and 1939 they were rebuilt as 2-8-2Ts, together with Nos 5255-5274, and 14 of the earlier engines numbered between 4202 and 4249, becoming the 7200 class. Until 1943 new front ends fitted to the 4200-99 and 5200-4 batches retained the original straight platform framing, but later re-cylindering included some with the raised platform of the 5275 series, as is seen here on No 4233, with curved drop ends and outside steam pipes./*Michael Hale*

Bottom left: No 5201, coasting with a down freight towards Pyle West Junction on the South Wales main line on July 4, 1955. Although this locomotive did not have outside steampipes, a circular patch is discernible on the smokebox side, showing a boiler change from a locomotive which was so modified./
S. Rickard

Below: No 5227 standing in for the train engine of the 12.20pm York-Swansea, which had failed at Llanwern, photographed at Cardiff on July 12, 1957. Such duties were a rarity for the class, which was specifically designed for short-haul coal traffic in South Wales, being limited in coal and water capacity. Outside steam pipes were fitted from the start on Nos 5205 onwards and the cylinder diameter was increased to 19in, giving a tractive effort of 33,170lb./*R. O. Tuck*

materialised (see Appendix 1). In fact, the batch of locomotives Nos 5275-94 built in the latter half of 1930 never ran in traffic as 2-8-0Ts and after initial running-in they were stored at Swindon until they were rebuilt as 2-8-2Ts. Nos 5255-74 were taken out of traffic for conversion. War-time traffic demands brought about a resumption of construction of the 2-8-0Ts in 1940, and new engines were numbered 5255-64 to replace those rebuilt as 2-8-2T. A final order for 10 locomotives, Nos 5265-74, was cancelled in 1941.

Although designed for use in South Wales, odd examples were allocated elsewhere for such purposes as banking, and St Blazey had them for china clay traffic — another example of short-haul duties.

The engines were built as follows:

No 4201	Swindon	1910
Nos 4202-4221	Swindon	1912
Nos 4222 4231	Swindon	1913
Nos 4232-4241	Swindon	1914
Nos 4242-4261	Swindon	1916-17
Nos 4262 4285	Swindon	1919-20
Nos 4286-4299		
5200-5204	Swindon	1921-23
4200		
Nos 4205-5214	Swindon	1923
Nos 5215-5244	Swindon	1924
Nos 5245-5274	Swindon	1925-26
Nos 5275-5294	Swindon	1930*
Nos 5255-5264	Swindon	1940

The series starting with No 5205, as depicted in the line drawing, were Collett's version of the design, with only minor modifications compared to the original.

First of class withdrawn: 4224 (1959)
Last of class withdrawn: 5235 (1965)
Example preserved: 5239

* Did not run as 2-8-0T (see Appendix 1).

4300 class 2-6-0
Mixed-Traffic Engines

Introduced: 1911
Total: 342
GWR classification: 4300, 5300, 6300,
7300 D, Blue; 8300, 9300 D, Red.
BR Power Class: 4MT

No prototype was considered necessary for this highly versatile and useful class of Moguls, which was basically a tender version of the 3150 class 2-6-2T of 1906, with the standard No 4 boiler. The design arose from Churchward's desire to have a new range of types to operate secondary services. At first some thought was given to using inside cylinders, but Holcroft was instrumental in changing his chief's mind on the subject. Holcroft had visited Canada, where he had been particularly impressed by the versatility of the Mogul type and when Churchward learned of this he instructed him to prepare plans for a new 2-6-0, with 5ft 8in wheels, outside cylinders and the standard No 4 boiler, using as many standard parts as possible. The new design was produced very quickly and an order for 20 locomotives was placed with the works. The class was to prove so successful, and equally at home on passenger and goods duties, that proposals for other medium-size standard types were shelved.

The 1914-18 War produced a demand for more of such versatile locomotives and the Moguls were produced in quantity, with Nos 5319-26/8-30 actually seeing war service in France, where they were sent (in ROD livery, but retaining their running numbers) in September 1917, returning to the GWR in April and May 1919.

The dimensions of the initial batch were as follows: The cylinders were $18\frac{1}{2}$in diameter by 30in stroke and drove coupled wheels of 5ft 8in diameter. The leading pony truck wheels

Below: The drawing depicts the final version of the class, introduced in 1932, when 20 new engines, Nos 9300-19, were updated by Collett with side-window cabs, outside steam pipes and screw reverse. In this form they were somewhat heavier and the boiler was pitched higher; the frames were lengthened at the rear by $6\frac{1}{2}$in.

Top right: No prototype was constructed for the 4300, as it was, in effect, a tender version of the 3150 class 2-6-2T. Instead, an initial batch of 20 locomotives was constructed in 1911. (Nos 4301-20) and these were the first *new* GWR locomotives to be delivered with top feed. No 4301 pictured here had the numberplates set lower on the cabsides than subsequent engines; early-style superheater damper on smokebox side; copper-capped chimney and tall safety valve bonnet in polished brass; lamp bracket on top of smokebox; and tall swan neck to front vacuum pipe. The enlarged centre splasher also housed the reversing lever, a feature of Nos 4300-5389./*Ian Allan Library*

Centre right: No 4321 of the second batch, 4321-40, of 1913 in fully lined green livery with copper capped chimney and polished brass safety valve bonnet. This, and all subsequent batches had the frames lengthened by 9in at the rear and had enlarged cabs. The two circular spectacle plates above the firebox were later removed from all classes of Churchward locomotives originally fitted./*Ian Allan Library*

Bottom right: Austerity plain green livery, with bright metal finishes painted over and works plate removed, on No 4304 of the pioneer batch of Moguls. Rainstrip added to cab roof, otherwise basically unchanged as seen here in immediate post-WW I days. The shorter cab of the original series can be seen by comparison with the photograph of No 4321. This was the Saint class cab, whereas No 4321 onward carried the County class cab, which provided more room on the footplate./*Ian Allan Library*

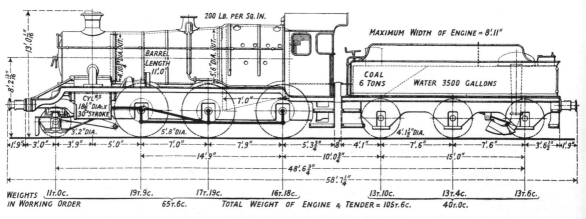

A classic Churchward combination! Class 4300 No 5378 piloting 2800 2-8-0 No 2841 on a freight bound for South Wales at Llannihangel Summit on September 13, 1952. Although photographed in BR days, the Mogul shows very little visual alteration since built. The chimney is of the cast-iron variety, the tall version of the safety valve bonnet is retained and the engine is in unlined black livery. The upper lamp bracket has been moved to the top of the smokebox door, a modification dating from 1936 onwards. In 1917 a modification had been introduced to obtain a better distribution of weight, which involved moving the pony truck fulcrum forward. This was applied from new to Nos 5320 onwards and earlier locomotives were brought into line./ *P. M. Alexander*

were of 3ft 2in diameter. The combined total heating surface was 1566.74sq ft comprised of a tube heating surface of 1228.02sq ft, a firebox heating surface of 122.92sq ft, and a superheater of 215.80sq ft. Boiler pressure was 200lb and the tractive effort was 25,670lb at 85 per cent. Standard 3500-gallon tenders were attached, and the total weight of engine and tender in full working order was 102 tons.

The second batch, Nos 4321-40, produced in 1913 had lengthened frames at the rear (to take a County-type cab) and an increased total heating surface of 1690.94sq ft. One problem which affected the class was weight distribution and a number of modifications took

place over the years, with the particular improvement of 1917 in which the pony truck fulcrum was moved forward.

Between 1936 and 1939 88 of the 4300 series and 12 of the 8300 series were withdrawn and certain parts including the wheels and motion were incorporated in Grange and Manor class 4-6-0s (see Appendix 1) as the first stage of a scheme to replace all the Moguls. The plan was curtailed by the outbreak of World War II and was not revived.

So wide was their range of activities that it would be easier to assess them as the true 'maids-of-all-work' of the GWR. There were, however, various restrictions upon them caused by severe curves (in Devon and

From No 5384, a modified design of motion-bar cross frame was fitted, and it can be seen on No 6320 pictured here, starting with No 5390, the right-hand splashers were modified to clear the reversing rod. A fine smoke effect is thrown skyward by No 6320 as it climbs Brewham Bank near Bruton with an up goods./*W. Vaughan-Jenkins*

Left: No 6372, seen here at Wiveliscombe Station, was one of several of the class which had automatic tablet changing apparatus on the tender side. The engine is waiting with the 11.45am from Taunton, while No 7333 (of the later side-window cab series) approaches with the 10.10am from Ilfracombe, on September 1, 1962./*R. G. Turner*

Bottom left: In 1921 an order was placed for 50 2-6-0s with Robert Stephenson & Co, a most unusual act for the GWR at the time, as it had constructed all its own locomotives for many years. In the event only 35 were actually built by the firm (Nos 6370-99 and 7300-4) and the remaining 15 (Nos 7305-19) were built concurrently at Swindon, using parts supplied by the Stephenson company. One of the Stephenson locomotives is seen here with a Leamington Spa-Evesham local passenger working at the top of Hatton Bank./*T. E. Williams*

Below: Experience with the standard Moguls in areas such as Cornwall, where sharp curves abounded, revealed that serious flange wear was occuring on the leading coupled wheels. Despite some early modifications to redistribute weight, the problem was tackled more drastically by increasing the weight at the front end. This was done by moving forward the bufferbeam by 12 inches and inserting a heavy casting, to bring weight to bear on the leading pony truck. First engines to receive the modification were Nos 4351/86/95/85 which were renumbered 8300/35/44/34 in late 1927, but for some reason they reverted to previous state almost immediately. In the first three months of 1928 65 engines of the 5300 series were modified and had 3000 added to their existing numbers, thus becoming 8300. In stages between 1944-1948 they were restored to original condition, regaining their original 5300 numbers, although 12 were replaced by Grange class 4-6-0s in 1937-39. No 8301 is seen here./*Collection A. Swain*

Bottom: Intermediate 3500-gallon tenders were attached to some of the Moguls during their careers, such as No 7315 seen here at Oxford on October 1, 1959. The locomotive has outside steam pipes and new cylinders, a modification first made to No 4327 in 1928, and applied as necessary to other locomotives over the years, while Nos 6362-6369 and 7320/1 were built new with them in 1925./*E. M. Patterson*

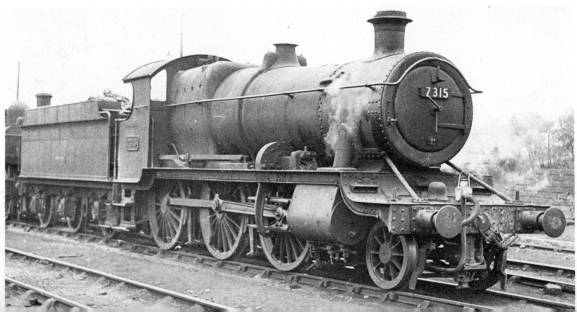

*See Appendix I

Top left: Collett produced 20 new Moguls in 1932, which were in effect updated Churchward locomotives. They were numbered 9300-19 and featured such refinements as screw reverse, side-window cabs, outside steam pipes and short safety valve bonnets. They had the heavy front end casting ahead of the running plate, introduced with the 8300 conversions, and weighed 65 tons 6cwt full, thereby confining them to Red routes. No 9317 was photographed working hard with the evening 6.57 goods from Southampton Docks to Cheltenham, the engine being on SR metals and working for the first time, as an example of the class, over the Andover road, on September 16, 1953./*G. Wheeler*

Centre left: The heavy bufferbeam castings were removed from the 9300 series between 1956-9, reducing their weight to 63 tons 17cwt full. This brought them down to Blue route restriction and they were accordingly renumbered 7322-41, in sequence. No 7337 (previously No 9315) is seen here leaving Dulverton with the 3.55pm Barnstaple-Taunton on June 22, 1963, with an Exe Valley train in the bay platform. This driver's side view of the locomotive shows the modified screw reverse, with housing in front of cab, introduced by Collett./*M. J. Fox*

Bottom left: Immaculate lined green BR livery and polished short safety valve bonnet on No 6374, fresh from overhaul at Caerphilly Works in July 1959. By 1948 when the class passed into BR ownership, the original total of 342 engines had been reduced to 241 as a result of replacement by 4-6-0s* and the withdrawal of No 6315 after accident damage. From late 1956 green livery was restored to the surviving engines, both lined and unlined versions appearing. The engine has received outside steam pipes and has the lamp bracket on the smokebox door./*G. Wheeler*

Below: A rear threequarter view of No 6384, built in 1921 and seen as running nearly 40 years later. The modified splashers (to clear reversing lever) and motion bracket frame are clearly visible. New cylinders and outside steam pipes were fitted in 1947. The engine was photographed at Bath Green Park shed, with unfamiliar companions in the shape of Fowler 2-8-0 No 53807 and 0-6-0 No 44557, on May 14, 1960. No 6384 makes a pleasing picture with clean unlined green livery./ *R. J. Blenkinsop*

Cornwall) which required special modification to weight distribution, as described in the captions to the illustrations.

The engines were built as follows:

Nos 4301-4320	Swindon	1911
Nos 4321-4340	Swindon	1913
Nos 4341-4380	Swindon	1913-15
Nos 4381-4399 } 4300	Swindon	1916
Nos 5300-5349	Swindon	1916-18
Nos 5350-5369	Swindon	1918-19
Nos 5370-5389	Swindon	1919-20
Nos 5390-5399 } 6300-6317	Swindon	1920-21
Nos 6318 6341	Swindon	1921
Nos 6342-6361	Swindon	1923
Nos 6362-6369	Swindon	1925
Nos 6370-6399 } 7300-7304	Rbt Stephenson & Co.	1921-22
Nos 7305-7319	Swindon*	1921-22
Nos 7320-7321	Swindon	1925
Nos 9300-9321	Swindon	1932

As mentioned, 100 engines were withdrawn for rebuilding in the period 1936-39. A further locomotive, No 6315, was withdrawn after being damaged in 1945 (Llangollen accident), but it was 1948 when withdrawals of life-expired engines started and examples of the class ran until November 1964.

First of class withdrawn: 4365/86 (1948)
Last of class withdrawn: 6364/7/95, 7318/ 20/7 (1964)
Example preserved: 5322

* Nos 7305-7319 were constructed at Swindon using parts supplied by Robert Stephenson and Company.

SECTION 12

4600 class 4-4-2T
Light Tank Engine

Introduced: 1913
Total: 1
GWR Classification: A, Blue

The success of his existing light 2-6-2T designs led Churchward to consider a 4-4-2T version with larger coupled wheels, which would enable it to run at higher speeds with local trains. He therefore produced No 4600 out of existing standard parts, and it was generally similar to the 4500 class except for the coupled wheels. Classed as a light suburban tank engine, it had cylinders of 17in diameter by 24in stroke and was fitted with 10in piston valves. The wheel diameters were bogie and trailing 3ft 2in, and coupled 5ft 8in. The total heating surface was 1271.86sq ft, comprised of a tube heating surface of 1178.01sq ft and a firebox heating surface of 93.85sq ft; the No 5 standard boiler first fitted had a working pressure of 200lb psi. The tank capacity was 1100 gallons and the bunker held 3 tons of coal. The weight in working order was 60 tons 12cwt. Tractive effort was 18,360lb.

When new the engine was sent to work in South Wales for a short period before transfer to the Birmingham area, where it spent the rest of its working life. No further engines followed the prototype and it seems that Churchward recognised that the 4-4-2 wheel arrangement with its low (only about half) weight available for adhesion, and with the restricted capacity of the water tanks, had not really improved upon a 4500 in terms of power or speed. For suburban traffic the larger and heavier 2-6-2Ts excelled in any case. As a solitary engine, its career was not a long one and it was an early Churchward régime withdrawal.

No 4600 was built at Swindon in 1913; it was withdrawn in 1925 and is not preserved.

Right: A most attractive little engine, No 4600 is seen here in works grey livery, for photographic purposes, and shows the engine as built. A later development was the fitting of a superheated boiler, and the front bogie pivot was moved forward 4in. Visually the engine was a great success, with curved framing at front and back and a pleasing copper-capped chimney. It was unique in being the only bogie engine to have the front end strengthening struts. Note also the unique location of the sandbox fillers on the leading ends of the side tanks./*British Rail*

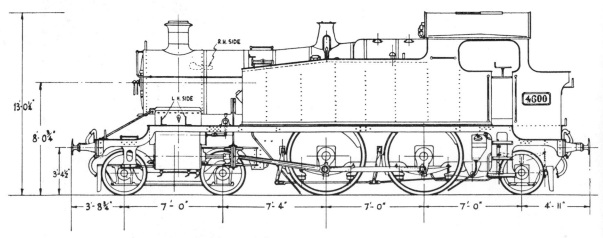

WHEELS—LEADING & TRAILING 3'-2" DIA 10 SPOKES
DRIVING 5'-8" DIA 18 SPOKES.

4700 class 2-8-0
Mixed-Traffic Engines

Introduced: 1919
Total: 9
GWR Classification: D, Red
BR Power Class: 7F

A request from the traffic department to provide an engine for working heavy but fast vacuum-fitted loads, which resulted in part from the success of *The Great Bear* on the Cocoa Train (see page 78) resulted in a decision by Churchward to produce an eight-coupled version of the 2-6-0 mixed-traffic engines with larger boiler. The standard No 1 boiler was in fact too small, whereas the solitary standard No 6 of the 4-6-2 was too large. For the prototype 2-8-0 Churchward therefore selected a No 1 boiler and provided a specially lengthened smokebox, to give the same overall length as would be needed for a new No 7 boiler, which was being designed specifically. The usual synthesis of standard parts resulted in the appearance of No 4700 in 1919.

As built, the engine had cylinders of 19in diameter by 30in stroke, coupled wheels of 5ft 8in and a leading pony truck of 3ft 2in. With the original No 1 boiler the total heating surface was 2171.43sq ft consiting of a tube heating surface of 1686.60sq ft, a firebox heating surface of 154.78sq ft and a superheater of 330.05sq ft. Boiler pressure was 225lb and tractive effort was 30,460lb at 85 per cent. The engine weighed 77 tons 14cwt and the tender 40 tons, giving a total

Below: The drawing illustrates the class after replacement of the original 3500-gallon tenders in 1932-33.

Top right: Churchward's final essay in new locomotive design, prior to retirement in 1921, was this mixed-traffic 2-8-0 with 5ft 8in wheels, which appeared in May 1919. It was an attempt to enlarge on the 4300 2-6-0s for extra heavy duties, by adding another pair of coupled wheels and using the standard No 1 boiler instead of the No 4 of the Moguls. In practice the No 1 boiler was not long enough for such a large machine, but in any case Churchward was working on a larger boiler in 1919 which he proposed fitting to the Stars, Saints, 2800 and 4700. Known as the standard No 7, only the 4700 Class in fact received it, as the Chief Civil Engineer objected to the weights in the other cases. No 4700 is shown here as originally built, with the standard No 1 boiler, which it lost in May 1921./*Ian Allan Library*

Centre right: The new standard No 7 boiler was provided in May 1921, and was considerably larger than the standard No 1 originally fitted. It was higher pitched, and outside steam pipes were added, with the snifting valves visible on the outside of the steam chests. The safety valve bonnet was, of necessity, of reduced height, but the maximum height at chimney was actually reduced compared to the original design. No 4700 is shown soon after re-boilering had taken place. The chimney was cast iron, and the top lamp bracket was on top of the smokebox. The vacuum pipe swan neck protrudes well above bufferbeam level, and the locomotive has a 3500-gallon tender attached./*Ian Allan Library*

Bottom right: Comparison with the foregoing picture of No 4700 shows No 4707 (seen here in post-war GWR livery, at Old Oak Common on March 23, 1946) to have been altered remarkably little over the years. The most obvious change is the 4000-gallon tender attached (dating from 1932-3), and the cab roof has been slightly extended at the back. The upper lamp bracket has been moved down to the smokebox door and the vacuum pipe swan neck lowered. The snifting valves were not placed on the steam chests on Nos 4705-8, being mounted instead in the standard position above the platform and behind the outside steampipes. A suggestion that the class should be named was turned down by the GWR Board of Directors in view of their mixed-traffic concept; only express passenger engines were named at that time (1922-3)./ *H. C. Casserley*

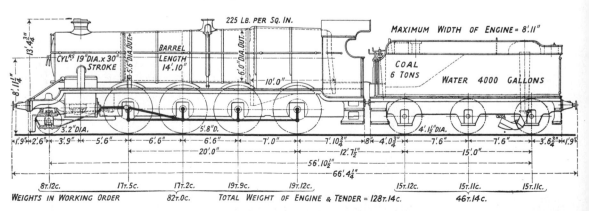

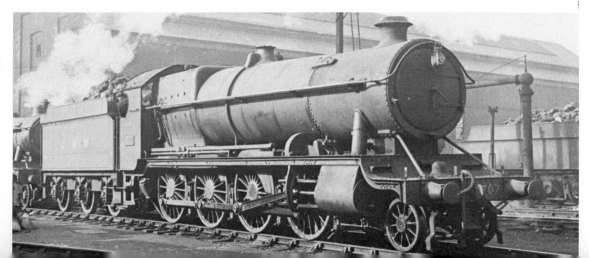

weight in full working order of 117 tons 14cwt. The tender capacity was 3500 gallons.

In May 1921 the prototype new standard No 7 boiler was ready and replaced the original on No 4700. The total heating surface was raised to 2556sq ft consisting of a tube heating surface of 2062.35sq ft, a firebox heating surface of 169.75sq ft and a superheater heating surface of 323.90sq ft. The grate area was increased from 27.07sq ft to 30.28sq ft. The overall weight of the engine and tender was 122 tons, with the engine now weighing 82 tons. Outside steam pipes were fitted.

The weight of the engines and their long coupled wheelbase, somewhat restricted their usefulness, and upon Churchward's retirement Collett did not increase their numbers, preferring to utilise his new Hall class mixed-traffic 4-6-0 design. Nevertheless they were outstanding performers, and most imposing to watch at speed.

The engines were built as follows:

| No 4700 | Swindon | 1919 |
| Nos 4701-4708 | Swindon | 1922-23 |

First of class withdrawn: 4702 (1962)
Last of class withdrawn: 4703/4/7 (1964)
None preserved.

Top left: A striking angle to view a 4700 2-8-0, emphasising the massive boiler dimensions. No 4706 was photographed at Reading on a Saturdays-only passenger duty. This clearly shows the automatic train control apparatus below the bufferbeam; also the front end struts, applied to these engines when new. A proposal to fit screw reverse to the class was made in the early 1950s, but not pursued./*C. B. Herbert*

Bottom left: In the plain black livery of early BR days No 4703 nevertheless makes an impressive picture as it ascends Dainton Bank with a down express freight in April 1954. Long-distance vacuum-fitted freight trains were the true *metier* of the class with the result that much of their work was performed during the hours of darkness./*D. S. Fish*

Bottom: Originally conceived as mixed-traffic engines, the 4700s were to be seen in BR days on express passenger duties between London and Devon, particularly at peak summer periods. Such was the case here, when No 4707 in clean BR black livery, was photographed working a Paddington-Kingswear express between Aller Junction and Torquay on August 27, 1955./*D. S. Fish*

Below: Resplendent in full BR passenger green livery, No 4703 was photographed at Swindon in May 1962. Apart from livery changes, the class underwent remarkably little outward alteration over the years. No 4703 retains the sniffing valves on the steam chests and the generally smart appearance belies its 40 years of service; in fact it was withdrawn just two years later. The highest mileage attained by an engine of the class was that of No 4705 with 1,656,564 to its credit when withdrawn in December 1963./*G. Wheeler*

Miscellaneous Designs of the Churchward Era

A brief summary of non-standard designs, railmotors, and conversions of existing engines.

Below left: In 1901 Swindon produced two 0-6-4 crane tanks for duties at the works. They were Nos 17 *Cyclops* and 18 *Steropes* and were basically 850 class 0-6-0 pannier tanks. A third engine, No 16 *Hercules*, was constructed as late as 1921. All three lasted until 1936./*H. C. Casserley*

Bottom left: Strangely numbered between the prototype two-cylinder 4-6-0 and the first French Atlantic was this solitary little 0-4-0T, No 101, which was built at Swindon in 1902. As first delivered it was an experimental oil-burning locomotive, with a highly unusual boiler design surmounted by a standard brass safety valve cover. This was replaced by a Lentz boiler in 1903, which carried a dome on the middle of three rings, and had rail-motor type Pop safety valves. later still, in 1905, the engine was converted to coal burning, the cab backplate was removed and a small bunker added. The locomotive is illustrated here in its final state. The engine spent its somewhat truncated working life shunting at Swindon, being finally withdrawn in September 1911./*Ian Allan Library*

Below right: Coincident with Churchward's succession to Dean at Swindon, was the upsurge of interest in the steam rail-motor on British railways, as a potential answer to the threat of the electric tramcar and motorbus. Early in 1903 the GWR borrowed a Drummond LBSC/LSWR joint East Southsea service rail-motor for trials between Stroud and Cheltenham. By October of the same year two new GWR rail-motors, Nos 1 and 2, were in service between Chalford and Stonehouse. They were a considerable advance upon the Drummond design; the locomotive portion was more powerful and was enclosed as part of the bodywork. By the following May further rail-motors of basically similar design, with high elliptical roof and slabsides with vertical matchboarding were in service. They were numbered 3-14, and were followed by Nos 17-28 in September. No 17 is seen here, with the engine portion at the right-hand end./*Ian Allan Library*

Bottom right: There were 99 rail-motors of varied design in service by 1908, including some 70ft long vehicles, and a number of specially constructed trailers. No 74, illustrated here, was built by the Gloucester C & W Co and was of the Branch type, with luggage accommodation and with the later more modern body with curved lower side panels, bow ends and lower elliptical roof (features of Nos 29-99). The trailers were similar in appearance and also featured the large gong above the driver's cab, operated by a pedal. The rail-motors encouraged traffic beyond their somewhat limited capacity — even when hauling a trailer — and their career was relatively shortlived. From 1915 onwards they were progressively rebuilt as auto-train trailers, by the simple means of converting the engine compartment to take extra seating and a luggage/guard compartment. However a few rail-motors remained in active service until the mid-1930s./*Ian Allan Library*

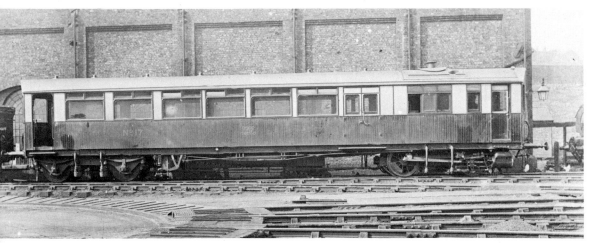

Right: A bizarre event in 1906 was the reappearance of four existing 0-6-0Ts completely enclosed in new dummy coachwork, for working auto-trains. They were painted brown and cream to match the trailers and must have presented an odd spectacle indeed, besides being most awkward to maintain. One is seen at Trumpers Crossing (for Osterley Park) Halte, (note the spelling of halt) coupled to a rail-motor type auto-trailer. The experiment was shortlived./*Ian Allan Library*

Below: A need for further 2-6-2Ts and a surplus of the 2301 Dean goods 0-6-0 class resulted in the appearance of 20 rebuilds from Swindon in 1907. The 0-6-0s Nos 2491-2510, which had been built in 1896, were rebuilt as 2-6-2T Nos 3901-20. Inside cylinders were retained and the frames were altered to take a standard pony truck at each end. Side tanks (with a cutaway for access to the inside valve gear) flanked a Churchward No 5 boiler, with tall safety valve bonnet and slender cast-iron chimney. This picture shows No 3902 in original condition, in shop grey livery, with overall cab and short bunker./*Ian Allan Library*

Below right: No 3908 is seen in later condition, with extended rear to the bunker, top feed, and a housing over the front pony truck springing. As many items as possible were of Churchward origin, but the class cannot really be considered as a standard design, being in essence a conversion from Dean practice. The engines were allocated to the Birmingham area to displace the 2-4-2T double-enders, as they offered greater adhesive weight./*Ian Allan Library*

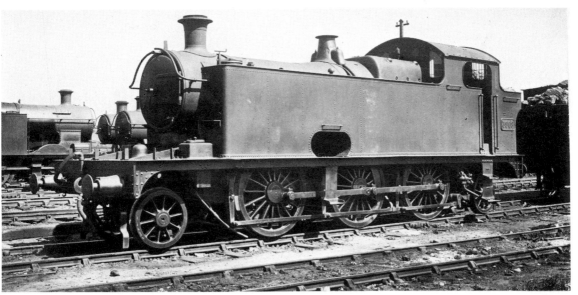

Above: Their short wheelbase allowed the 1361 class 0-6-0ST to operate on docksides and wharves where the curves were too severe for larger shunting engines. Although produced with as many details as possible adhering to Churchward's current practice, these engines were in fact a non-standard design, drawn up by Holcroft, and their basis was the life-expired ex-Cornwall Railway 0-6-0ST design, which Holcroft modernised. Introduced in 1910, the five locomotives were Nos 1361-5, and proved most reliable and useful. No 1361 is seen here in shop grey livery. The small pipes above the cylinders were not outside steam pipes, but part of the exhaust passage./ *Collection B. Haresnape*

Right: A clear view of the sloping bunker fitted to all five of the class (a somewhat similar bunker was tried out on 2-6-2T No 4515) 0-6-0ST No 1363 works a transfer freight from Laira MPD to Tavistock Junction, past Laira Junction signalbox on August 30, 1961./*R. C. Riley*

Above right: Another view of No 1363 at Laira Motive Power Depot, taken on September 25, 1956 with King class 4-6-0 No 6025 *King Henry III* and an unidentified BR Standard Britannia Pacific, in the background. The engine does not have the toolbox which some carried on the footplate, but carries a BR smokebox numberplate. It had otherwise altered remarkably little over the years./*H. C. Casserley*

Appendix 1

Subsequent Rebuilds of Churchward Locomotives

SECTION 1, page 24
2900 class 2-cylinder 4-6-0 (Saint class)
No 2925 was rebuilt by C. B. Collett, with 6ft diameter driving wheels and a side-window cab, in 1924. This was the prototype of the Hall class.

SECTION 7, page 64
4000 class 4-cylinder 4-6-0 (Star class)
Between 1925-29, the following engines were dismantled and converted to the Castle class 4-6-0, by Collett: 4000/9/16/32/7. They retained the same running numbers. In the period 1937-40 Star class 4-6-0s Nos 4063-4072 were taken out of stock for similar conversion. In this case they reappeared with new numbers 5083-5092, in the same order.

SECTION 9, page 78
No III. 4-cylinder 4-6-2 *(The Great Bear)*
In January 1924 this famous engine was dismantled at Swindon for reconstruction as a Castle class 4-6-0, due to the inner firebox of the unique No 6 boiler requiring renewal. The locomotive was renamed *Viscount Churchill*.

SECTION 10, page 82
4200, 5205 class 2-8-0T
A decline in the South Wales coal traffic led to the decision to widen the usefulness of the redundant 2-8-0Ts by converting them to 2-8-2T, with a bunker capacity almost equal to that of a tender engine. In 1934 Nos 5275-5294 were rebuilt to become Nos 7200-7219 of the new 7200 class. They were followed in 1935-36 by Nos 7220-7239, which were rebuilt from Nos 5255-5274. The final batch, known as the 7240 class, appeared in 1937-

Pioneer GWR four-cylinder express passenger locomotive No 4000 *North Star*, in final form, as a Castle class engine, with side-window cab and attached to a flush-sided Hawksworth tender. The post-Churchward locomotives of the GWR will form the subject of a companion volume, to be published later, entitled *Collett and Hawksworth Locomotives./G. Wheeler*

39 and were rebuilt from the older 4200 series of 2-8-0Ts, in the following order: 4239/ 4220/4202/4204/ 4216/4205/4234/ 4244/ 4249/4209/4219/ 4240/4210/4245, which took the numbers 7240-7253 in that sequence.

SECTION II page 86
4300 class 2-6-0 Mixed-Traffic
Between 1936-39, 88 of the 4300 series and 12 of the 8300 series Moguls were withdrawn and the wheels and motion were used in the construction of new 4-6-0s; 80 Grange class and 20 Manor class. The boilers were retained where condition warranted it, as spares. The scheme was to convert all the 2-6-0s, but the outbreak of World War II prevented it.

The full story of the development of Churchward's standardisation scheme, under the auspices of his successors C. B. Collett and F. W. Hawksworth, will be the subject of a companion volume *Collett and Hawksworth Locomotives* now in preparation.

Appendix 2

Named Locomotives

Listing all named Churchward locomotives, with their original, and subsequent numbers, with the exception of the Dean/Churchward 4-4-0 classes and the French Atlantics. Where more than one name was carried they are listed in chronological order.

4-4-2*/4-6-0 4000 Class (The Stars)
(see page 64)

40*; 4000	North Star
4001	Dog Star
4002	Evening Star
4003	Lode Star
4004	Morning Star
4005	Polar Star
4006	Red Star
4007	Rising Star; Swallowfield Park (1937)
4008	Royal Star
4009	Shooting Star
4010	Western Star

*originally 4-4-2, converted to 4-6-0

4011	Knight of the Garter
4012	Knight of the Thistle
4013	Knight of St Patrick
4014	Knight of the Bath
4015	Knight of St John
4016	Knight of the Golden Fleece
4017	Knight of the Black Eagle; Knight of Liege (1914)
4018	Knight of the Grand Cross
4019	Knight Templar
4020	Knight Commander
4021	King Edward; The British Monarch (1927)
4022	King William; The Belgian Monarch (1927)†
4023	King George; The Danish Monarch (1927)†
4024	King James; The Dutch Monarch (1927)†
4025	King Charles; Italian Monarch (1927)†
4026	King Richard; The Japanese Monarch (1927)†
4027	King Henry; The Norwegian Monarch (1927)
4028	King John; The Roumanian Monarch (1927)†
4029	King Stephen; The Spanish Monarch (1927)
4030	King Harold; The Swedish Monarch (1927)†

† Names removed in 1940/1.

4031	Queen Mary
4032	Queen Alexandra
4033	Queen Victoria
4034	Queen Adelaide
4035	Queen Charlotte
4036	Queen Elizabeth
4037	Queen Philippa
4038	Queen Berengaria
4039	Queen Matilda
4040	Queen Boadicea
4041	Prince of Wales
4042	Prince Albert
4043	Prince Henry
4044	Prince George
4045	Prince John
4046	Princess Mary
4047	Princess Louise
4048	Princess Victoria (temporarily Princess Mary, 1922)
4049	Princess Maud
4050	Princess Alice
4051	Princess Helena
4052	Princess Beatrice
4053	Princess Alexandra
4054	Princess Charlotte
4055	Princess Sophia
4056	Princess Margaret
4057	Princess Elizabeth
4058	Princess Augusta
4059	Princess Patricia
4060	Princess Eugenie
4061	Glastonbury Abbey
4062	Malmesbury Abbey
4063	Bath Abbey
4064	Reading Abbey
4065	Evesham Abbey
4066	Malvern Abbey; Sir Robert Horne (1935); Viscount Horne (1937)
4067	Tintern Abbey
4068	Llanthony Abbey
4069	Margam Abbey; Westminster Abbey (1923)
4070	Neath Abbey
4071	Cleeve Abbey
4072	Tresco Abbey

Standard Churchward nameplate and numberplate, applied to Star class 4-6-0 No 4004 *Morning Star*, with Egyptian serif brass lettering. The Swindon works plate below the nameplate on the centre splasher was removed from 1911 onward on all the locomotives./*Ian Allan Library*

4-6-0/4-4-2* 2900 Class (The Saints)
(see page 24)

100; 2900	Dean; William Dean (1902)
2901	Lady Superior
2902	Lady of the Lake
2903	Lady of Lyons
2904	Lady Godiva
2905	Lady Macbeth
2906	Lady of Lynn
2907	Lady Disdain
2908	Lady of Quality
2909	Lady of Provence
2910	Lady of Shalott
2911	Saint Agatha
2912	Saint Ambrose
2913	Saint Andrew
2914	Saint Augustine
2915	Saint Bartholomew
2916	Saint Benedict
2917	Saint Bernard
2918	Saint Catherine
2919	Saint Cecilia; Saint Cuthbert (1907)
2920	Saint David
2921	Saint Dunstan
2922	Saint Gabriel
2923	Saint George
2924	Saint Helena
2925	Saint Martin
2926	Saint Nicholas
2927	Saint Patrick
2928	Saint Sebastian
2929	Saint Stephen
2930	Saint Vincent
2931	Arlington Court
2932	Ashton Court
2933	Bibury Court
2934	Butleigh Court
2935	Caynham Court
2936	Cefntilla Court
2937	Clevedon Court
2938	Corsham Court
2939	Croome Court
2940	Dorney Court
2941	Easton Court
2942	Fawley Court
2943	Hampton Court
2944	Highnam Court
2945	Hillingdon Court
2946	Langford Court
2947	Madresfield Court
2948	Stackpole Court
2949	Stanford Court
2950	Taplow Court

* originally 4-4-2, converted to 4-6-0

2951		Tawstock Court
2952		Twineham Court
2953		Titley Court
2954		Tockenham Court
2955		Tortworth Court
171*;	2971	Albion; The Pirate (1907); Albion (1907)
172*;	2972	Quicksilver; The Abbot (1907)
173;	2973	Robins Bolitho
174;	2974	Barrymore; Lord Barrymore (1905)
175;	2975	Viscount Churchill; Sir Ernest Palmer (1924); Lord Palmer (1933)
176;	2976	Winterstoke
177;	2977	Robertson
178;	2978	Kirkland; Charles J. Hambro (1935)
179*	2979	Magnet; Quentin Durwood (1907)
180*;	2980	Coeur de Lion
181*;	2981	Ivanhoe
182*;	2982	Lalla Rookh
183*;	2983	Red Gauntlet; Redgauntlet (1915)
184*;	2984	Churchill; Viscount Churchill (1906); Guy Mannering (1907)
185*;	2985	Winterstoke; Peveril of the Peak (1907)
186*;	2986	Robin Hood
187*;	2987	Robertson; Bride of Lammermoor (1907)
188*;	2988	Rob Roy
189*;	2989	Talisman
190*;	2990	Waverley
98;	2998	Vanguard; Ernest Cunard (1907)

4-6-2 No III
(see page 78)

III The Great Bear

4-4-0 3800 Class (The Counties)
(see page 56)

3473;	3800	County of Middlesex
3474;	3831	County of Berks
3475;	3832	County of Wilts
3476;	3833	County of Dorset
3477;	3834	County of Somerset
3478;	3835	County of Devon
3479;	3836	County of Warwick
3480;	3837	County of Stafford

End of the line for three Churchward engines, 4700 class 2-8-0, No 4701 and two 2800 class 2-8-0s, Nos 2842/52, are hauled dead to Sharpness Docks, for cutting up, by 0-4-2T No 1445 on July 20, 1964./B. J. Ashworth

3481; 3838	County of Glamorgan		County of Chester (1907)
3482; 3839	County of Pembroke	3815	County of Hants
		3816	County of Leicester
3801	County Carlow	3817	County of Monmouth
3802	County Clare	3818	County of Radnor
3803	County Cork	3819	County of Salop
3804	County Dublin	3820	County of Worcester
3805	County Kenny	3821	County of Bedford
3806	County Kildare	3822	County of Brecon
3807	County Kilkenny	3823	County of Carnarvon
3808	County Limerick	3824	County of Cornwall
3809	County Wexford	3825	County of Denbigh
3810	County Wicklow	3826	County of Flint
3811	County of Bucks	3827	County of Gloucester
3812	County of Cardigan	3828	County of Hereford
3813	County of Carmarthen	3829	County of Merioneth
3814	County of Cheshire;	3830	County of Oxford

Bibliography

The following books, which were referred to in the course of compiling this pictorial history, are recommended to the reader desiring further information about G. J. Churchward and his locomotives.

Cook, K. J.   *Swindon Steam,* Ian Allan Ltd.
Holcroft, H.   *An Outline of Great Western Locomotive Practice, 1837-1947,* Ian Allan Ltd.
Maskelyne, J. N.   *Locomotives I Have Known, Further Locomotives I Have Known,* Percival, Marshall
Nock, O. S.   *GWR Steam,* David & Charles *British*
Poultney, E. C.   *Express Locomotive Development, 1896-1948,* Allen & Unwin *The*
RCTS   *Locomotives of the Great Western Railway* (published in 12 parts), Railway Correspondence and Travel Society *G. J.*
Rogers, Col H. C. B.   *Churchward, A Locomotive Biography,* Allen & Unwin *Great Western Album*
Riley, R. C.   *(Nos 1 and 2),* Ian Allan Ltd.